Victorian Sheet Music Covers

KU-520-110

Victorian Sheet Music Covers

Ronald Pearsall

David & Charles: Newton Abbot

By the same author
Worm in the Bud (Weidenfeld & Nicolson)
The Table-Rappers (Michael Joseph)

ISBN 0 7153 5561 9

HERTFORDSHIRE
LIBRARY SERVICE
741·64
0353173

© RONALD PEARSALL 1972
All rights reserved. No part of this
publication may be reproduced, stored
in a retrieval system, or transmitted,
in any form or by any means, electronic,
mechanical, photocopying, recording or
otherwise, without the prior permission
of David & Charles (Publishers) Limited

Set in 11 on 13 point Bembo
by C E Dawkins (Typesetters) Ltd London SE1
and printed in Great Britain
by Latimer Trend & Company Limited Whitstable
for David & Charles (Publishers) Limited
South Devon House Newton Abbot Devon

CONTENTS

FOREWORD

Victorian sheet music covers are a fascinating mirror of an age, a special kind of ephemera that lifts up a corner of a hidden canvas, providing us with a glimpse of an almost vanished era. They reflect the times far more assuredly than the fashionable academic pictures of the 1860s and 1870s.

We cannot really claim that these covers are great art. But the experiments in typography reflect a restless striving for novelty, while the use of lithography demonstrates how new technologies were being used in the service of mass communication. The songs themselves have their own appeal—sentimental, cynical, and often very witty; they were the love songs and social comment of the otherwise silent masses, the audience of the great music halls that spread through London and the provinces to an extent that is almost unbelievable today.

Over the last few years there has been an increasing interest in sheet music covers as collectible items, but little research has been done on them, and almost nothing has been written on the artists involved in what was really big business. The music covers shown in this book are typical of those that can be found with just a little searching. In the selection of sheet music covers for this book a policy has been decided upon to include covers of historical and technical interest rather than those that are merely attractive. It would have been easy to cram the book with immaculate covers by Concanen and Brandard and ignore the cruder examples by lesser artists and anonymous journeymen.

But many of the latter have a naivety and charm that it would be a pity to pass by, and although many of them can hardly be called great art they have a distinction as a kind of bygone in which their very faults have a part to play. They have never been reckoned *objets d'art*, and consequently they have come down to us grubby and woe-begotten.

Even their promoters considered them disposable. We find covers with their edges snipped off by the printer's guillotine, with colours overlapping, and some even printed by broken plates. Yet even these specimens add to our knowledge of a long-neglected genre that is only now beginning to receive the attention it deserves.

ACKNOWLEDGEMENTS
Plates 27, 33, 36, 38, 44 and 45 are reproduced by courtesy of John Hall and David Macwilliams; 18, 31 and 41 by courtesy of the Victoria and Albert Museum; 8 by courtesy of Edward Casassa; and 26 by courtesy of Graham Webb.

1 THE EARLY DAYS

The earliest known music illustration was to the title page of Luther's 'German Mass', engraved by Hans Cranach in 1526. In 1611 the first music for the virginals, 'Parthenia', had an engraved cover by William Hole. Hole (fl 1600-30) was the first English engraver of music on copper plates. This cover may have been an English first, but is of no great artistic consequence, portraying a girl sitting at the virginals. For some reason Hole has given her only four digits on each hand.

Until the early nineteenth century, pictorial music covers are uncommon. They were invariably engraved, and although most of them are of not much interest there are a few that were hand-coloured in a most beautiful manner and would command high prices were they to turn up in the open market.

Then three events occurred almost simultaneously—the growth of popular music, the invention of lithography, and a sudden upsurge of interest in typography. Lithography was invented by accident by Aloys Senefelder (1771-1834), a composer, a violinist, a poet, a painter and an engraver. Having no money to buy copper plates for engraving, he tried using the surface of the local stone.

The principle of lithography, without which there would be no art of the sheet music cover, is that grease repels water, while calcareous limestone takes both. A drawing is made upon the stone with an ink or a crayon of a greasy composition, and is washed over with water which sinks into all parts of the stone not protected by the drawing. A roller charged with ink is then passed over the stone. The drawing receives the ink, but the water-soaked stone left blank is not affected. This was the basis of the art, and from this point Senefelder progressed to colour lithography.

Senefelder obtained the patent rights for his invention in Bavaria, joined up with a music-seller named André, and after a lithographic press had been established in the town of Offenbach-on-Main, André's brother and

Senefelder came to London to negotiate an English patent. The art was introduced into England in 1800 under the name of polyautography, and in 1803 André published a collection of prints by T. Stothard and other artists under the name *Specimens of Polyautography*. This was the first lithographed book published in England.

The man who did most for the new art in Britain was Rudolph Ackermann. Born in Saxony in 1764, Ackermann had been a saddler and a coach-builder in Paris and London, but in 1795 he established a print shop and drawing school in the Strand. An enterprising man, Ackermann had in 1801 patented a method for waterproofing paper and cloth, and had set up a factory for this purpose in Chelsea. His shop formed part of the first house in London to be lit by gas.

He translated Senefelder's book *A Complete Course of Lithography*, established a printing press, and bought a quarry in Germany for raw materials. Ackermann immediately began to use his lithographic press, publishing his *Repository of Arts, Literature, Fashions, &c.* monthly until 1828. He also pioneered the popular English annuals, beginning in 1825 with *Forget-Me-Not*. Despite the influence of Ackermann, there was still intense prejudice against the new medium. In a review of Captain Franklin's narrative of his polar expedition, the *Quarterly Review* solemnly warned the public against the 'greasy daubs of lithography', and it would seem that the British government thought lithography un-English, for they imposed an almost prohibitive duty on the importation of the stones.

Colour lithography had been investigated by Senefelder but it was not until 1837 that a patent for chromolithography was taken out by Engelmann. Probably the first use of chromolithography in an English musical publication was in 1841 in the annual *The Queen's Boudoir*.

In a sense, lithography had only been an alternative to the sophisticated forms of engraving such as mezzotint, the texture of which had a subtlety impossible to rival, but with the coming of chromolithography a great new vista was opened. For the first time multi-coloured work

1 (opposite)
'Olga' by Jullien, illustrated by John Brandard. Although Brandard worked in a variety of styles, this represents his most sought-after period, and collectors must expect to pay a high price for such covers. This waltz was of the early delicate kind, as can be seen by the demeanour of the dancers.

JULLIEN'S Celebrated Valses a Deux Tems. 4.th SET.

OLGA

OR THE
PRINCESS WALTZ,
COMPOSED & DEDICATED TO HER IMPERIAL HIGHNESS
THE GRAND DUCHESS OLGA,
BY
JULLIEN.

PRICE 4/

could be produced in quantity and cheaply—from 2,000 to 5,000 prints could be made from one stone.

In chromolithography every colour has a different stone, and for the better examples of this art, seen in illuminated gift books of the 1850s and 1860s but rarely in sheet music covers, as many as thirty stones were used. The reason for this is that stone can only give three gradations—the solid, the half-tint, and the quarter-tint. Work of the highest quality may need two or three blues, with yellows, reds, greys and browns in proportion. With this in mind it is obvious that the greatest problem in chromolithography is correct registration, ie getting the stones into exactly the right position so that the colours do not overlap. Registration is a good test of quality, for sloppy workmanship soon reveals itself.

Putting together a chromolithograph was rather like a jigsaw. The medium was very suitable for subjects with outlines, for the outlines in one colour served as an infallible guide to the registration of the other colours. Stones could wear or the surface could break up. This was not such a disaster as might appear, as it would have been for a copper plate to have been damaged, for the damp print from the stone could be matched against a fresh stone to serve as an easy guide for renewal. It was not likely that all the stones would fail together, and the pieces of design from the existing good stones would act as a key to registration for the new piece.

The method of renewing a stone was the same in single-colour lithography—using a fresh print against a new stone to provide the design information necessary for the application of inks. In the long runs of best-selling sheet music there is no indication which were first, second or third editions.

The vulnerability of the stone was the only major snag of lithography, far outweighed by the advantages—the cheaper initial cost compared with the older methods of reproduction; suitability for subjects of large size such as posters; suitability for subjects with outlines; and the capacity for printing on almost any paper. This had a great appeal for music publishers turning out large editions of ephemera.

12

2 (opposite)
'Swiss Quadrille' by Jullien, an extremely fine cover of 1847, using nine different type founts, including the marvellous Tuscan variant for 'Swiss'. Written by Jullien, published by Jullien, performed by Jullien, sold by Jullien, perhaps it is only to be expected that the cover bears his signature as well.

JULLIEN'S

SWISS

QUADRILLE,

Dedicated to Mrs JOHN SAINSBURY, Vansitart House, Greenwich

as Performed at the Author's Concerts

Theatre Royal Drury Lane,

by his Celebrated Orchestra.

ARRANGEMENTS OF THE DESCRIPTIVE MUSIC IN THE SWISS QUADRILLE, AND SWISS MELODIES.

Nº 1 _ THE SWISS QUADRILLE _____ 4/-		Nº 3 _ THE STORM, AVALANCHE & FINALE _____ 3/-	
2 _ THE INTRODUCTIONS, & RANZ DES VACHES } 3/-		4 _ THE SWISS GIRL *as Sung by* MISS DOLBY 2/6	
as Performed on the ALPEN HORN *by* KŒNIG			

Ent. Sta. Hall.

Nº 1, Price 4/-
DUET 4/-

LONDON,

Published by JULLIEN & COMPANY, Royal Musical Conservatory & Musical Library.

214. REGENT STREET. & 45. KING STREET.

Where may be had all the

VOCAL & INSTRUMENTAL MUSIC PERFORMED AT THESE POPULAR CONCERTS.

Jullien

Lithography was fortunate in that it was born fully grown, and that as soon as chromolithography was patented only one further improvement seemed necessary —the stone itself. Stone was cumbersome—one firm which specialised in lithographic printing, Day & Son, kept 800 tons in stock at any one time—and could sometimes be unreliable. The quality of stone first used by Senefelder, discovered by him at the village of Solenhofen in Bavaria, was unsurpassed. The stones came out in large sizes, 3–5in thick. As lithography spread in popularity throughout Europe—Gericault and Ingres contributed to its acceptance as a high art medium—other sources were needed. Stone was found in France, Spain, Italy and Greece but it did not compare with the Bavarian material. Fear that the supply of Bavarian stone would run out, plus the fact that the Bavarian quarries were owned by peasants with a sharp eye for the main chance, led to the search for a substitute for stone in which the principle of grease repelling water would still function. The earliest substitute was zinc, but the grease and the water only penetrated the surface to a slight extent; a more suitable medium was found to be treated zinc. Zinc was either oxidised or coated with a composition that emulated stone. Fortunately the quarries of Bavaria proved all but inexhaustible, and were being mined well into this century.

The next landmark is 1844 when Louis Antoine Jullien began to issue a series of polkas and quadrilles lithographed by John Brandard in colour[1]. John Brandard is often confused with his brother Robert, who was an engraver specialising in topography.

1844 was the year in which 'Jullien began that strange mixture of good, bad, and indifferent selections, which took hold of the public immediately and served in the first direction to improve the taste and enlarge the knowledge of the rising generation' (*Musical Recollections*, J. E. Cox, 1872). In 1838, Jullien (1812–60), a conductor and composer of dance music, had fled from Paris on becoming insolvent; in 1840 he assisted an English violinist, Eliason, in promoting a series of *Concerts d'été* at Drury Lane Theatre.

3 (opposite)
'Valse d'Adieu' composed by Jullien for his last series of Promenade Concerts. The artist of this fine black and white on buff lithograph was John Brandard, and the portrait is of Jullien himself in suitably pensive mood. This is an excellent likeness as well as being a superb picture.

VALSE D'ADIEU.

A FAREWELL TO ENGLAND.

COMPOSED

BY

JULLIEN.

PRICE

This was a stepping-stone for Jullien. His aim was to provide orchestral concerts at the cheapest price for the greatest number. He instigated a series of promenade concerts at the Royal Zoological Gardens, Surrey Gardens and the Lyceum, in which music by Haydn, Mozart and Beethoven rubbed shoulders with polkas and quadrilles composed and arranged by Jullien for bands of eccentric and mammoth proportions. 'M. Jullien broke down the barriers and let in the crowd', commented *The Musical World* in 1859.

He used a band of ninety players and a chorus of eighty, and kept the programmes topical by producing each season a new monster quadrille. He did not hesitate to update the classics, love them as he unquestionably did. The storm movement of Beethoven's *Pastoral* Symphony had an obbligato part for a player shaking a tin box full of dried peas.

A master of showmanship, Jullien conducted Beethoven with a specially jewelled baton and spotless white kid gloves brought to him on a silver salver. His coat-tails flew about his legs, his hair fell into his eyes, and at moments of especial excitement he would seize a violin or piccolo and add to the noise, after which he would collapse elegaically into a velvet chair placed there for the purpose.

His public loved him, a public that cut across the social strata, a public that feted him and wished to buy his quadrilles and polkas for home performance as solo piano pieces (price 4 shillings)[2] or as piano duets (price 5 shillings). Jullien promoted the pictorial sheet music cover as no one else could have done. Despite the insipid content of the music, the covers are beautifully executed and printed[3]. They have status, as Jullien himself had on the rostrum, and are dedicated to this or that princess. *Punch* referred disparagingly to him as 'The Mons', but whatever the traditionalists thought of him he made an indelible mark on British musical life, building up the mass audience that Sir Henry Wood was to capture sixty years later for his promenade concerts.

He may have been a trifle mad. His ambitions included setting the Lord's Prayer to music. 'Imagine the title

4 *(opposite)*
'*La Brunette et la Blonde*' by G. W. Rohner, cover by John Brandard. Presumably an attempt to exploit the European Market, the main titles are in French while the picture caption is in English. Black and white on buff was a common colour scheme for well-executed landscapes in the English easel painting tradition. The lack of connection between the cover subject and the music content is strong enough to excite comment.

5 *(overleaf)*
'*Ducking's Row*' by Lucy Ann Rhensherl, an interesting early lithograph by John Brandard in an unfamiliar comic style. Such covers were considerably earlier than his popular covers for Jullien, and this one is technically interesting in that it demonstrates how a graphic artist of Brandard's attainments could use lithography in a style that seemingly cries out for engraving. Note the superbly drawn butcher's boy. In such covers as these, the distinction between art and ephemera is lost.

LA BRUNETTE, ET LA BLONDE.

St. GOAR, ON THE RHINE.

DEUX VARSOVIENNES ALLEMANDES.

Nº 1   LA BRUNETTE____ in E♭

2   LA BLONDE_____ in F

PAR

C. W. ROHNER.

There's Mifs Le Blanc, each day, around her house, collects a crowd,
By playing airs from operas, while I play twice as loud,
And open all the windows, too, as far as e'er they'll go
But Music's not worth list'ning to, it seems, in ⸻

⸻ DUCKING'S ROW,
WRITTEN BY
LUCY ANN RHENSHERL,
ARRANGED BY
S. NELSON.

Pr. 2/-

LONDON, JEFFERYS & NELSON, SOHO SQUARE.

Sir Roland Gower,

ROMANCE

OF THE

DAYS OF KING RICHARD.

BY

CHARLES BLONDEL.

Ent: Sta: Hall.   Price 2/-

LONDON

Chas. W. Manby, 85 Fleet Street

page,' he said, 'music by Louis Jullien, words by Jesus Christ.' In 1856 Covent Garden Theatre burnt to the ground and Jullien lost all his music including the manuscripts of his monster quadrilles and polkas. He returned to Paris and in 1859 was thrown into a debtors' prison, dying the following year in a lunatic asylum muttering to Berlioz—whom he promoted in Britain when no one else would touch him—that he had 'a cosmic A passing through his ears'.

The artist who designed the sheet music covers for Jullien's quadrilles, waltzes and polkas was John Brandard. Brandard was in his thirties, a dandy and a fop like Jullien, an experienced lithographer who had done fancy title pages for 'Books of Beauty' and ladies' pocket books. Again, like Jullien, he was a perfectionist and kept two assistants to make certain that the surfaces of the lithographic stones were as smooth as it was humanly possible to get them. Note the finish of [4]. He was perhaps the most meticulous of the lithographic artists employed on music covers, and for his work he was well paid—20 guineas (£21) a title. It is rather out of character that he did comic covers as well [5].

This money was paid by Jullien, for these works were published by his own firm, Jullien & Company, Royal Musical Conservatory and Musical Library, of Regent Street and King Street, London. These addresses not only served as points of sale for the music, but as centres of adulation.

Jullien was a twentieth-century man born ahead of his time, knowing the commercial value of self-dramatisation and clever promotional methods. His composing and publishing of quadrilles and polkas was shrewd, for at that time carpet-dancing, ie ballroom dancing, was becoming very popular. Queen Victoria was in her mid-twenties and was very keen on dancing. Polkas were particularly delectable, and a craze known as polkamania spread through the country. Polkas were also combined with mazurkas in one dance [7].

Another factor that contributed to the success of Jullien's sheet music was the popularity of the piano. 'The first half of the nineteenth century was above all the

6 (previous page)
'Sir Roland Gower' by Charles Blondel. The cover is an interesting amalgam of styles, an accomplished anonymous lithograph surrounded by a self-consciously picturesque Gothic border, with a curiously inappropriate use of the Rustic type face made famous by Dicky Doyle from about 1840.

7 (opposite)
'The Tivoli Polka Mazurka' by W. Vandervell, lithographed by T. Packer. Known as 'the graduated tint Packer' on account of the subtle qualities of his skies, this admirable Italian landscape owes nothing to the title, and is in the tradition of English easel painting rather than the sheet music cover. The unusual type face used is very close to the charmingly named Pretty face of 1862.

THE
TIVOLI POLKA MAZURKA.

COMPOSED BY

W. VANDERVELL.

Pr. 3/-

LONDON.
PUBLISHED BY, B WILLIAMS, II. PATERNOSTER ROW.

age of the pianoforte', wrote Richard Nettel in 1948, and there seems no need to question this. Liszt had made his first London appearance in 1827, and in 1832 Mendelssohn had published his first book of *Songs Without Words*, almost certainly the best-selling piano music of the nineteenth century. In the 1840s the piano recital was introduced; a leading exponent was Arabella Goddard who features on music covers[8]. It is perhaps unnecessary to state that all the sheet music that concerns us contains a piano part, either as principal or as accompaniment. Without the piano and people to play it there would have been no sheet music as we know it.

It is commonly assumed that the amateur pianists of the Victorian period were either young ladies for whom piano playing was a status symbol or an escape from sexual inhibitions, or clergymen. This is not true. Pianomania, like polkamania, touched all classes, and young men, either from the middle or artisan classes, did not consider it effeminate to take up this instrument. Being able to play the piano was a distinct asset in genteel courtship, for not only could the executant exhibit hidden talents without swank but could also, when playing duets with his or her beloved, indulge in some saucy flirting. It will be noticed in popular piano duets for the amateur market how frequently the hands cross over irrespective of the needs of the music.

The development of the piano also played a major part in the vogue. In 1777 Robert Stodart had created a 'new invented sort of instrument, or *grand pianoforte*, with an octave swell'; in 1795 his son William was granted a patent for a 'new invented *upright grand pianoforte* in the form of a book-case', and in 1820 the same firm developed the revolutionary principle of metallic bracing. Until then it was almost necessary to have a piano-tuner living on the premises, so much did the wooden frame respond to temperature and humidity.

The up-and-coming middle-classes were able to have an instrument which was both status symbol and piece of furniture. In 1827 Pleyel exhibited a small upright piano, and the interest aroused caused Erard to evolve the same thing in 1831, the year that also saw the vital

8 (opposite)
'Miss Arabella Goddard's Pianoforte Repertoire.' Miss Goddard (1836-1922), one of the first lady pianists to gain an international reputation, retired in 1878. This very accomplished portrait is unsigned. The studied pose indicates that the artist worked from a photograph.

MISS ARABELLA GODDARD'S PIANOFORTE RÉPERTOIRE.

A CORRECT EDITION

OF THE

PIECES PERFORMED BY THAT DISTINGUISHED ARTIST

1	ERIN, FANTASIA ON IRISH MELODIES	J. BENEDICT.	4/-
2	CALEDONIA, FANTASIA ON SCOTCH MELODIES	J. BENEDICT.	4/-
	COMPOSED EXPRESSLY FOR MISS ARABELLA GODDARD.		
3	HOME SWEET HOME	THALBERG.	3/-
4	LILLIE DALE	THALBERG.	4/-
5	THE LAST ROSE OF SUMMER	THALBERG.	4/-
6	ALBION, FANTASIA ON ENGLISH MELODIES	J. BENEDICT.	4/-

Nº 6   Price 4/-

innovation of overstringing. This may sound technical, but it is simply that the bass strings cross over the tenor or upper strings to get greater length and therefore greater sonority than if the strings were all parallel. The implications of this are clear: it was now possible to have small pianos with all the tone of a grand.

Pianos for the masses began about 1840 with the ubiquitous cottage piano. This is now a term of reproach, but initially they were adequate instruments, though with the advent of the £10 piano many of the developments such as overstringing and crisp actions were forgotten. Too much money was spent on a gaudy and showy case. Nevertheless even these pianos helped to foster the love of music that existed throughout all levels of society; the German sneer that England was the land without music was the mis-statement of all time.

2 THE GOLDEN AGE

Important as Jullien was in the evolution of the pictorial sheet music cover, he was of less consequence than the social phenomenon of the music hall. The ancestor of the music halls that spread throughout London and the provinces and were the most lively manifestation of working class mores and thought of the century was Evans's. Evans's was the home of glee and madrigal, and although women were not officially allowed they 'could lurk unseen behind a grill, as in the House of Commons, listen to choir-boys in Eton collars warbling "The Chough and Crow", and "Blow gentle Gales", and watch their male friends supping on sausages and mashed and bottled stout'. Evans's, presided over by 'a host of the older school', was eminently respectable. After the madrigalists were exhausted, a singer named Henry Sidney told the world to 'jog along as it will' insisting that he would be 'free and easy still', while another regular, Herr van Joel, gave imitations of farmyard animals, a form of entertainment that persisted until World War 2.

Marginally less respectable was Charles Sloman, 'the only English improvisatore' who sang doggerel verses alluding to the dress, manner or deportment of any member of the audience who happened to strike his notice. He wrote many songs, and worked most of the music halls. His set piece was 'The Wolf' ('Locks, bars, and bolts are rent asunder').

Contemporary with Evans's were the various saloons, such as the Eagle in the City Road, dating from 1839, and the Royal Britannia Saloon at Hoxton. There were also the clubs, frequented by 'baby bucks, blacklegs, and half-pay officers', with their Tavern Concerts, and the notorious Cider Cellars in Maiden Lane, and Coal Hole in Fountain Court, Strand. All these had their speciality singers known by one or two distinctive songs which they adopted; some of these singers, on account of the sauciness or blasphemy of their songs, were barred from the more respectable places. W. G. Ross, whose song 'Sam Hall' with its 'damn you all' refrain may still evoke

9 (overleaf)
'Now I Love Sukey Dearly', a negro ballad in the Musical Bouquet series. Nigger minstrel songs became popular in the 1830s with the enormous fame of 'Jim Crow' Rice, who had his debut at the Surrey Theatre in 1836, later one of the first music halls, antedating Uncle Tom's Cabin *by sixteen years. In 1842, on Rice's second visit, 'in the fashionable collonade, in the filthiest street, in the naked, damp cellar and the luxuriously carpeted drawing-room, the words and tune of Jim Crow are constantly to be heard'. Although the engraving of 'Now I Love Sukey Dearly' is unsigned, it could be attributed to G. E. Madeley, who specialised in Nigger minstrel songs.*

MUSICAL BOUQUET

NEGRO

SONGS

"NOW I LOVE SUKEY DEARLY."
(FAVORITE NEGRO BALLAD.)

Now I lub Sukey dearly But Sukey won't lub me: If Sukey lub an o_der I can't see who he be

Sukey dear, Sukey dear, wont you cum and lib wid me, Sukey dear, Sukey dear, wont you cum wid me!

Nº 21.

THE CELEBRATED ELFIN WALTZES.
COMPOSED BY LABITZKY.

Musical Bouquet. Nos 181 & 182.

I. S.

memories after 130 years, was welcomed at the Cider Cellars but banned from Evans's.

The singers in the clubs and saloons were the old-time ballad singers changing with the age and moving indoors, and they did not hesitate to hawk their music from table to table. As late as 1861 there were no less than 700 ballad singers in London. It was, declared the *National Review*, 'an ancient if no longer honourable profession'.

The music cover before 1844 lacks the style and polish of the later 'classic' issues. There is an uneasy compromise with the engraved music titles of the late eighteenth century, and there is great use of half-titles, the pictorial part of the cover occupying the top, and the music starting half way down the sheet[9]. Nevertheless, these titles are extremely interesting historically, and many talented graphic artists, such as Ashley[10 and 11], plied their engraving tools for the edification of the habitués of Coal Hole and Cider Cellar. Even Brandard, the artist for the Jullien covers, engraved covers and half-covers for this market.

A distinction can be made between the sheet music produced for the clubs and saloons and the broadsheets issued by the ballad press, the principal printer of which was Catnach. These broadsheets were lyrics without music, printed on brightly coloured paper on old wooden presses. They were pictorial in the sense that if a printer had any blocks that were marginally apposite they would be used at the head of the sheet.

The broadsheets specialised in racy scandal and 'orrible murder. The authors received 1 shilling a copy, or a meal and a dozen copies to hawk around. Catnach retired in 1838 and died in 1841, but the ballad presses went on well into the 1870s. In 1871 there were four ballad presses, the most prominent of which was Henry Disley's of 57 High Street, St Giles, the notorious Seven Dials area swept away when New Oxford Street was built. Disley took over the mantle of Catnach and continued to specialise in murder and sex.

A barman in the dock quarter of London who turned out to be a woman received the full ballad treatment, as did the murderess Mrs Maybrick:

10 (previous page)
'The Celebrated Elfin Waltzes' by Labitzky, illustrated by Alfred Ashley. This belongs to a series known as the Musical Bouquet. Ashley was a contemporary of Brandard but used engraving rather than lithography as his chosen medium. He worked in the style of Dickens's illustrator, Phiz, but he had a genuine streak of phantasy akin to that of Richard Doyle or Richard Dadd.

11 (opposite)
'The Maniac', composed and sung by Henry Russell. Russell, born in 1812, was a popular singer in the saloons and song and supper rooms that preceded the music hall, and was famous for moral ballads. 'The Maniac', illustrated by Alfred Ashley, brought his rather macabre doom on himself. Ashley was also a painter of calm sedate landscapes, exhibiting in London between 1850 and 1853.

28

THE MANIAC.

GRAND SCENA COMPOSED AND SUNG BY

HENRY RUSSELL.

Then to each gay and flirty wife may this a warning be,
   Don't write to any other man or sit upon his knee;
When once you start like Mrs Maybrick perhaps you
   couldn't stop,
   So stick close to your husband—keep clear of Berry's
   drop. [ie the hangman's scaffold]

Despite the raffish atmosphere of the clubs and saloons, this was an entirely different world from that of the ballad press. Dickens and Thackeray frequented Evans's and the Coal Hole. Dickens only went to Seven Dials in search of journalistic copy, and it was a brave man who went there alone. There was a curious Victorian occupation called 'minders' who were strong-arm men and escorted sensation-seekers at their own request into the slums of 'the Dials'.

To some degree there was a cult of the club and saloon singer such as Henry Russell, but it was not until the end of the 1840s that entrepreneurs looked about for a new angle, based upon the increasing popularity of the singer and the song. The clubs and saloons were small and limited. In November 1848, Richard Preece of the Grand Harmonic Hall at the Grapes, Southwark Bridge Road, renamed it the Surrey Music Hall. It was the first use of the name music hall. Charles Morton took the Canterbury Arms, Upper Marsh, Lambeth, enlarged it to take 700 people, and the Canterbury Music Hall was born.

Many other people jumped on the band waggon. The Mogul Saloon in Drury Lane was renamed the Middlesex Music Hall in 1851, and throughout the 1850s and 1860s music halls proliferated—Wilton's in 1856, the South London Palace in 1860, the Bedford, Camden Town in 1861, Deacon's of Clerkenwell in 1861, Collins's of Islington (the last to go) in 1862. In 1861 Morton bought the Boar and Castle at the junction of Tottenham Court Road and Oxford Street, and created perhaps the best known of the halls, the Oxford Music Hall, 94ft long, 41ft high.

The bulk of these halls were without proscenium and stage. The entertainment was presided over by a chairman who sat at a long table and hobnobbed with the audience. In response to the vast audiences the music halls were

12 (opposite)
'Love and Pride' was a comedy duet written by Harry Clifton for himself and Fanny Edwards, a harmless domestic disagreement written for the more respectable music hall audience:
She: Don't talk of marriage
   Unless in a carriage
   To church you can take me and
    make me your wife.
   You have not a shilling,
   Of course I'm not willing.
He: Then wretched I'll be all the days
   of my life.
The cover is by Henry Maguire the younger, the most prolific by far of the three Maguires engaged in music cover illustration.

LOVE AND PRIDE,

COMIC MEDLEY DUETT.

Mʀ HARRY CLIFTON, ᴀɴᴅ MISS FANNY EDWARDS.

IN THEIR NEW ENTERTAINMENT OF

RAGS ᴀɴᴅ TATTERS.

MOMUS ᴀɴᴅ APOLLO.

LONDON, HOPWOOD & CREW, 42, NEW BOND Sᵀ

getting, many halls were adapted. In 1860 the Alhambra was fitted out with proscenium and stage, in 1869 the South London Palace was likewise converted, followed by the Oxford in 1873.

The most important figure in the music hall scene was the singer, the centrepiece was the song, and a whole race of singers, principally male, sprang up to cater for the demand for quick-moving racy ditties, pertinent comments on various contemporary events, or the occasional sentimental ballad. These men were the pop idols of their time. They were paid upwards of £100 a week, provided by the music hall proprietors with carriages and horses, idolised by their audiences, and presented to posterity on innumerable sheet music covers.

Four of these men stand head and shoulders above their colleagues—George Leybourne who operated at the Royal, Holborn and the Canterbury; Arthur Lloyd at the Pavilion; G. H. Macdermott at the Pavilion; and the 'Great' Alfred Vance at the Oxford. Leybourne had gained his experience at 'free-and-easies' in the Midlands, and was said to have been once an engine-fitter in Newcastle. He made his first appearance in London at the Canterbury.

Arthur Lloyd, son of a Scottish comedian, was trained as an actor. He arrived in London about 1862 and made his debut in Islington. Lloyd was a man of parts, could write his own words and music and was responsible for a four-act play, *Bally Voyan*. G. H. Macdermott, also known as 'the Great Macdermott', had been a labourer, and after a spell at sea he became a popular favourite at the Grecian Theatre under the name of Gilbert Hastings. He too wrote a play, *Fair Rosamund*.

Macdermott had an aggressive and commanding presence, and was free with the *double entendre*; eventually this idolised star was barred from the West End, whereupon he bought a string of music halls in the East End and died a rich man, a rare event, for most of the singers—the Lions Comique as they were collectively called—died drunk and broke. Macdermott specialised in references to current events; in the song that brought him his first hit, 'The Scamp', there is mention of the Mormon, Brigham

32

13 (opposite)
'Folly and Fashion' was a companion piece to 'Love and Pride', and demonstrates Henry Maguire's skill in depicting interior scenes. The portraiture is excellent. These two actors are demonstrably the same people who appear on the cover of 'Love and Pride'. Maguire was extremely adept at using a limited colour range (the fewer the lithographic stones, the cheaper the end product), and 'Folly and Fashion' is white and black on buff.

14 (overleaf)
'Tableaux Vivants', by Charles Osborne, cover by H. G. Banks. Tableaux vivants were a rather dubious form of entertainment that could be described as Victorian striptease; Banks's insets on this cover, however, are saucy rather than salacious. R. G. Knowles was a music hall star who never quite reached the heights of his contemporaries.

FOLLY AND FASHION,
OR
Mr AND Mrs WRIGHT.

COMIC DUETT.
SUNG BY
MISS FANNY EDWARDS, AND Mr HARRY CLIFTON,
AT HIS
POPULAR CONCERTS IN GREAT BRITAIN AND IRELAND.

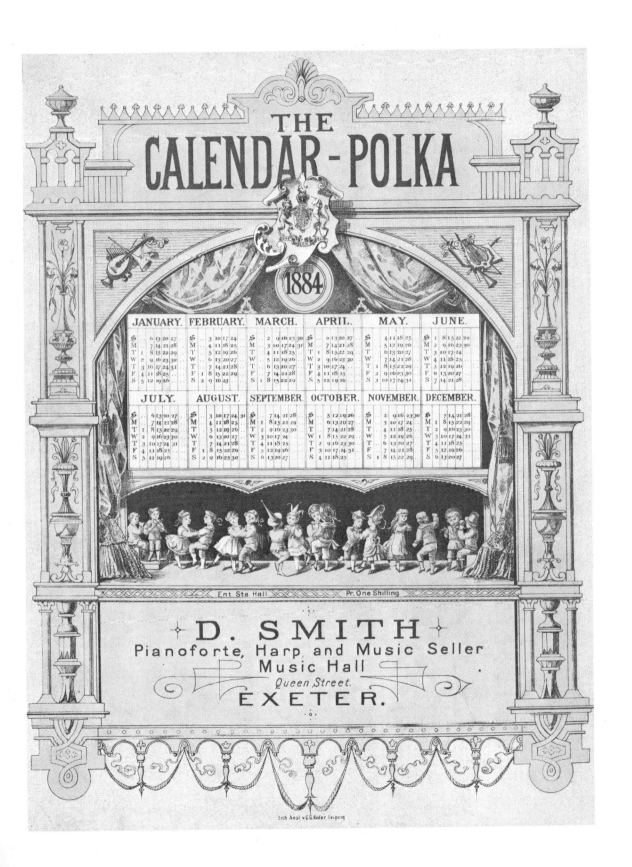

Young, as well as of Sir Roger Tichborne, the central figure of a celebrated court case. Macdermott gave a new phrase to the English language—'We don't want to fight but by Jingo if we do. . . .'

The last man of this quartet, the 'Great' Vance, is perhaps the most remarkable of them all. Born in 1840, he was a circuit actor in Preston and Northamptonshire, performing in Shakespeare and strenuous one-man shows in which he played twenty different parts at one performance. He made his first appearance in London about 1864 at the Metropolitan, Edgware Road. He was the first to portray a stage portrait of the period swell—fair hair, monocle, faultless evening dress. Versatile and a man of consequence, Vance could impersonate a coster-monger with his 'Chickaleary Bloke', sing a moral song such as 'Act on the Square, Boys', and turn on a rip-snorting performance with 'Clicquot, Clicquot, that's the Wine for Me'. His death is rather sad; in a barrister's wig and gown he was singing a topical song at a suburban hall, the Sun in Knightsbridge, when he collapsed after the refrain to the gallery, 'Are you guilty?' He was dead when the other members of the company got to him.

The common factor of these four men was presence. They dominated the rest of the bill, and the audience as well. There existed an empathy between singer and audience, brought to hysteria by clever innuendo and by spoken 'business' between the verses, that one would find difficult to parallel today. They were all in the £100 a week bracket, and lived up to it. Lloyd had a penchant for managing theatres which lost him most of his earnings. Vance and Leybourne were not only swells on the stage; their music hall persona extended into the world outside. When they died or retired from the halls something was lost, and their contemporaries such as Harry Clifton[12] and [13] and successors such as Charles Coborn (debut 1886), Dan Leno (1885), Albert Chevalier (1891) and R. G. Knowles[14] lacked the charisma of this endearing quartet. Their faces do not constantly turn up on sheet music covers as their predecessors' do.

That these later music hall stars lacked the magnetism

15 (previous page)
'The Calendar Polka' by A. Thompson McEvoy has a charming anonymous lithographed cover. By 1884 provincial music-sellers such as D. Smith of Exeter were realising that if they wanted to promote music they could not afford to use the prestige London printers such as Stannard. It was much cheaper to use German printing firms, especially Leipzig houses. The cost of 'The Calendar Polka' was 1 shilling; had it been printed in Britain it would hardly have cost less than 3 shillings (though it was usual to offer the music at half price soon after publication). The three-colour lithography (red, green and brown) also kept the price down.

16 (opposite)
'The Rink Galop', by Charles d'Albert, cover by Alfred Concanen, a marvellous lively cover celebrating the vogue for roller-skating. At any one time, Charles d'Albert had more than two hundred titles in the music-sellers' catalogues, and could always be relied upon to react to a topical theme. Waldteufel's 'The Skater's Waltz' was written for roller-skating, not, as is often thought, for ice-skating.

THE RINK GALOP

AS PERFORMED AT THE
ROYAL AQUARIUM WESTMINSTER

BY

CHARLES D'ALBERT

Pr 4/
Orchestra 3/-
Septett 2/-

of Vance, Macdermott, Lloyd and Leybourne was perhaps due to the changed conditions. Music hall was no longer intimate, no longer the logical extension of the saloons, the free-and-easies, the Coal Hole and the Cider Cellar, for in 1878 a law was passed; from that date, music halls needed a Certificate of Suitability, calling for a proscenium wall dividing the stage from the auditorium, and with this a safety curtain. The smaller halls could not afford the expense, and even the famous halls of twenty years earlier went under, including the Surrey Music Hall and Wilton's. Two hundred music halls in Britain closed. Quite as serious to the welfare of the music hall was the decision to ban liquor from the auditorium.

In the early music hall the sale of drink subsidised the entertainment. At the Canterbury admission was by a sixpenny refreshment ticket, and although this did not entirely pay for the turns it almost did, and it was several months before the owner made a charge of threepence admission (to any part of the house). Ladies' Nights were extremely popular at the Canterbury, except with the proprietor, for he maintained that the ladies interfered with the 'wet money'.

Music halls whose finances were threatened by the 1878 law clubbed together and syndicates were formed. From these sprang the chains of Empires, Palaces and Hippodromes that were such features of the provincial scene. Fewer but larger music halls replaced the small intimate halls, but it was still a booming business and no expense was spared in the decor and construction; their honest vulgarity makes an interesting parallel with the cinema in the 1920s and 1930s.

The London Pavilion, still with us in its modified form, its interior still telling its music hall ancestry, was a characteristic music hall of the age of syndicates. Opened in March 1885, it was converted in 1886, the tables were abolished along with the role of chairman, tip-up seats were installed, and in every respect it was like a straight theatre. The music hall had achieved parity with the other art forms and although reformers, including the celebrated Mrs Chant, considered that the promenade at the back of the stalls was the haunt of prostitutes—and she

17 (opposite)
'The Excursion Train' by W. Van-dervell has a cover by Concanen at his lively and inventive best. A brilliant stroke is the use of the front of the train as a surround for the delightful genre scene. The song itself was the kind of saucy, fast-moving ditty that the music hall audiences loved; the music was borrowed from other sources, but the lyrics have a precision and a gay wit that exemplifies all that was best in music hall song ("Tis the merry month of May, When twelve feet Posters meet your eye'). Despite the appearance of colour, Concanen used only three colours in this cover: red, green, and black.

38

THE
EXCURSION
BRIGHTON
BRIGHTON
A TENDER
TRAIN.
NARRATIVE.
SUNG BY
E. MARSHALL.
AT THE CANTERBURY HALL
Ent. Sta. Hall.
Price 3/-
WRITTEN EXPRESSLY FOR HIM BY
W. F. VANDERVELL.
MUSIC ARRANGED BY
WILLEM VANDERVELL
CONCANEN & LEE LITH.
STANNARD & DIXON, IMP.
LONDON
J WILLIAMS, 123, CHEAPSIDE

was right—the patronage of royalty, including the Prince of Wales, set the seal of approval on the music hall.

Nevertheless, the decline of the music hall can be detected in the late 1870s, though few were aware of it at the time. One can see this falling off in the quality of the songs; tuneful and memorable as the late Victorian songs are, they lack the bite and wit of the earlier ones. They are the mirror of the improved working class, and most were disposable. No one rushed out to buy the sheet music of tame insipid ditties as they had when Vance, Macdermott and Lloyd were in their glory.

This is not to say that the break was as clean as that. Many of the songs of the later years are still in the repertoire, such as Charles Coborn's 'Two Lovely Black Eyes', Katie Lawrence's 'Bicycle Made for Two' of 1892, or 'Get Your Hair Cut' of 1891. But the days of audacious ad libbing and salacious commentary on the scandals of the time were gone for good. Marie Lloyd (born 1870) was hauled before a watch committee on account of the lewd overtones she gave 'Come Into the Garden, Maud'. The condescending patronage of the minor nobility, the moral attitudes of the lower middle classes, an increasingly powerful force, succeeded in making the music hall a family entertainment.

Many of the songs of the 1850s, 1860s and 1870s did not wear very well. They were hitched to current events which would be out of the public mind in a month or two, though this did not matter when so many songs were being published. Songs such as 'The Exhibition of 1862' could not expect to cut much ice in 1863 or the 'Calendar-Polka 1884' in 1885[15]. 'Lounging in the Aq' would not mean much when the Westminster Aquarium had closed down. Much the same applies to the 'Rink Galop'[16]. In 1877 there was a popular song called 'Zazel'; in 1880, would anyone know who Zazel was? She was, in fact, a woman shot from a cannon in Westminster Aquarium. It might be mentioned that the Westminster Aquarium was never in its brief life greatly concerned with fish.

If song titles of the great years of sheet music covers were ephemeral, why did people buy them? And who did

18 (opposite)
'It is Never Too Late To Mend', an 1865 play based on Reade's 1856 novel, used this poster by Thomas Lee to advertise it. Although basically a decorative artist and an adder of inessentials, especially for Concanen, it is interesting to see Lee working on his own.

19 (overleaf)
'The Great Eastern Polka' by C. Coote, junior (composer of 'Mugby Junction Galop', and 'Somebody's Luggage Lancers') is an example of how composers seized upon contemporary events to which to tie a song or tune. 'The Great Eastern' was launched in 1874 and was chiefly used to lay underwater cables, but the polka was used in a burlesque of Aladdin. The anonymous artist of this cover has used an interesting kind of shorthand, so that this lithograph has almost the appearance of a modern print, though the odd sailing boat in the foreground is evidence of technical shortcomings or indecent haste.

40

ROYAL PRINCESS'S THEATRE
EVERY EVENING
EVERY EVENING
FROM PHOTO BY W. WALKER & SONS, 64 MARGARET ST CAVENDISH SQ W.
THOS W. LEE, LITH 65 CASTLE ST OXFORD ST
IT IS NEVER TOO LATE TO MEND.

SOLO 3/-

THE GREAT EASTERN POLKA

DUET 4/-

PERFORMED WITH THE GREATEST SUCCESS IN THE BURLESQUE OF ALADDIN AT THE STRAND THEATRE.

OH, COME WITH ME

WRITTEN BY

RICHARD RYAN

ADAPTED TO A FAVORITE MELODY

with Symphonies & Accompaniments

BY

JAMES CLARKE.

AUTHOR OF THE CATECHISM OF THE RUDIMENTS OF MUSIC,
EXERCISES IN HARMONY, HARMONIC COMPASS, &c &c

ENT. STA. HALL.   Pr. 2/.

LONDON. MESSRS R. COCKS & Cº. PUBLISHERS TO HER MOST GRACIOUS MAJESTY, 6, NEW BURLINGTON ST.

buy them? They were bought because it was the smart thing to do; they were bought by people who would not be seen dead in a music hall; they were bought because imitation swells thought it grand to imitate the Lions Comique, and they were bought because the tunes were catchy and the lyrics witty.

They were advertised widely in such weeklies as the *Illustrated London News*, and were sold from the publisher's shop or from the music shops that spread throughout London. In 1888, a typical year, there were nearly a hundred music shops in London: 15 in the City, 43 north of the river, 37 south of the river. The covers were ideally suited to display, and the windows of the music shops were completely covered with these covers, one in each rectangle of glass (plate glass was available but was prohibitively expensive).

To encourage big sales the publishers sometimes put out their music at an inflated price, and immediately advertised it at half-price. And big sales there were; a best seller such as Arthur Lloyd's 'Not for Joe' sold 80,000 copies, and when one considers figures like this it is not to be wondered at that music publishers were willing to employ first-rate artists on the covers at £20 a title. A good cover was its own advertisement, commanding attention in the music shop window.

The artist's fee and the cost of the art work for the cover constituted much of the outlay. The words of the song were obtained for very little, and inferior paper was used. The music came even cheaper, adapted from some standard tune in the repertory or pirated, such as 'The Excursion Train'[17]. George Leybourne's most popular song was probably 'Champagne Charlie' written by Alfred Lee (not to be confused with Thomas Lee, the artist[18]). When he came to London with the manuscript, Lee found it difficult to raise the toll then asked of all pedestrians who crossed Waterloo Bridge. The publisher Sheard advanced him £20 on the song, which was exceptionally generous for the time. Lee would have been glad to get £5; other lyric writers even less.

Dozens of publishers were involved in this lucrative business, perhaps the most important being Hopwood &

20 (previous page)
'Oh, Come with Me' by Richard Ryan 'with symphonies and accompaniments by James Clarke' is an example of an English publisher using a German lithographic firm to print the music. The illustration, signed by the monogram R.P.C., has a certain charm.

21 (opposite)
'Canti Popolari' by Carlo Graziani-Walter, a lesson in how not to use lithography, and how a passably competent cover design is wrecked by grotesque typography.

Alla Gentil Signorina Adelina Fanton

CANTI POPOLARI

PUBBLICAZIONE MUSICALE POPOLARE

DI

CESBIAVANNI

MAESTRO

Canto e Chitarra
Cent. 15

Proprietà degli Editori

ROVITO e LOCARTI
FIRENZE

Canto e Pianoforte
Cent: 20

N° 2

Crew of New Bond Street which published the songs made profitable by Leybourne and Vance. Only one of these has survived to this day, Chappell, which wisely diversified its interests, making pianos, promoting classical concerts and publishing a wide range of music. Invaluable archive material was lost in a fire at Chappell's in 1964. Francis, Day & Hunter entered the popular sheet music field in 1877.

Many of the publishers of music hall songs were of the get-rich-quick faction, and their work is shoddy and scamped. In 1888 there were sixty lithographic printers in the London area, all clamouring for work, and they were willing to cut their prices to the bone to survive. As the Mr Chappell of the day said, all a lithographic printer had to do was to set up an old press in a barn and he was in business.

The work of the cheap printers is characterised by poor registration, with the lithographic colour overlapping, by fading images (using the stone too many times and cutting down on the ink), and by a casual use of the guillotine. Frequently the title of the music itself is cropped off by the blade—[19] is a near thing.

The lithographic printers most prominent in sheet music covers of the 1860s and 1870s were Stannard. This name appears as Stannard & Co, Stannard & Son, and Stannard & Dixon. Some publishers who wanted quality covers and were anxious to jump on the band waggon found it cheaper to use German lithographic printers rather than the prestigious London houses[20].

The quality of German lithography is as good as that of the London firms; this cannot be said of French and Italian commercial lithography, as will be seen from the illustrations[21]. It is interesting to speculate on why this should be. The chief reason is that Germany was the recognised centre of music publishing, and firms such as Schott of Leipzig had branches in London and other European cities. Schott used the best lithographers available whether they were in Britain or Germany, being able to afford this because their market was international.

Schott and similar continental publishers had an edge over firms that specialised in music hall song covers such

22 (opposite)
'Ton Ame' by Aug. Tarry and Jos. Mth. Ht. Beltjens. A Belgian/German co-production, with a cover illustration in very much the English style.

23 (overleaf)
'Romante Romanesci' by Theodor Georgescu, published in Bucharest, printed in Leipzig, with text in Italian, this piece indicates the wide coverage of nineteenth-century popular music, and the great international interest in national music, provided that it was watered down acceptably, whether it was in high art (Brahms' 'Hungarian Dances', or Dvorak's 'New World' Symphony) or in potboilers such as 'Romante Romanesci'. British music hall songs lacked this European appeal, and consequently many minor publishers went out of business during the Victorian period.

DÉDIÉE À Mr. J. A. TUYN.

TON AME
MÉLODIE
Paroles de Mr. Aug. Tarry
Musique de
JOS. Mth H. BELTJENS
Op. 4.

Lyre Française No. 217.

Propriété des Editeurs Enregistré aux Archives de l'Union

Pr. 36 kr.

MAYENCE
ANVERS ET BRUXELLES
chez les fils de B. Schott.

Dépôt général de notre fonds de Musique à Leipzig, chez C. F. Leede, à Vienne, chez H. F. Müller.

ROMANȚE
Românesci

de

THEODOR GEORGESCU.

Proprietatea Editorului

CONSTANTIN GEBAUER, BUCURESCI.

Furnisor al cúrti.

Lith. Anst. v. F. W. Gorbrecht, Leipzig.

ROSALINE.

WRITTEN BY
J. H. ECCLES.
COMPOSED BY
George Barker.

Ent Sta Hall

Pr 2/6

LONDON,
CHAPPELL & Cº 49. & 50. NEW BOND STREET.

as Hopwood & Crew. The music hall was a specifically British phenomenon, and even in the United States it is difficult to find an exact parallel.

What type of music did Schott and the other German publishers issue? Briefly, that type that might be called popular drawing-room music, the equivalent of the polkas, quadrilles and waltzes made popular by Jullien. This kind of music, widely published of course in Britain as well, transcended national frontiers, and we come across curios such as a piece published in Rumania, printed in Germany, with titles and text in Italian[23]!

Drawing-room ballad was another outlet for publishers and music cover illustrators[24][25][26], but a distinction was made between general purpose ballads and songs from early Victorian English opera, such as 'Home, Sweet Home' and 'I Dreamt That I Dwelt in Marble Halls', and Sunday ballads. It was considered blasphemous for Sunday ballads to be given pictorial covers. It is also difficult to find classical music with such covers; it would have diminished the prestige of not only the music but the performer, and even the covers of gaudy showpieces for drawing-room pianists are without picture interest.

24 (previous page)
'Rosaline' by J. H. Eccles and George Barker. Concanen is in a rare elegaic mood, and there is a splendid use of subtle half-tones and quarter-tones in a composition, the basic colour of which is rose.

25 (opposite)
'Shells of Ocean or I Wander'd on the Sea Beat Shore' by J. W. Lake with music by J. W. Cherry. The use of a still-life group as the subject of a music cover is unusual.

26 (overleaf)
'The Murmur of the Shell' by the Hon Mrs Norton, published in 1861, has an almost horribly compelling cover. The expression on Miss P. Horton's face would seem to indicate that she is thinking of taking legal action against the anonymous illustrator. The packed texture of this fascinating cover, and its rich tones, demonstrate the capabilities of lithography.

SHELLS OF OCEAN,

OR

I WANDER'D ON THE SEA BEAT SHORE,

A SONG

WRITTEN AND INSCRIBED TO

P. FRASER ESQ?

BY

J.W. LAKE,

THE MUSIC COMPOSED BY

J.W. CHERRY.

Pr 3/-

ENT. STA HALL.

LONDON.

Published by HOLLOWAY & C?. 41, Hanway Street.

OXFORD ST.

STANNARD & DIXON IMP.

THE MURMUR OF THE SHELL

MISS P. HORTON IN HER ILLUSTRATIONS

BALLAD

SUNG BY

MISS P. HORTON,

WRITTEN & COMPOSED BY

THE HON^BLE MR^S NORTON.

3 WORDS AND MUSIC

Music hall songs may be divided into three classes: comments on the contemporary scene such as [27]; love songs such as [28]; and uplift songs such as [29]. They appealed specifically to an urban audience, and the nearest they got to the country was the Thames and the pleasure-gardens at Rosherville, Highbury Barn, Vauxhall and Cremorne. This audience was a sharp and knowing one from the inner suburbs of London and the East End, and the songs were directed with unerring skill, based on sure knowledge of the attitudes and interests of this audience.

The range of the current events mentioned in the song titles of the classic period of music covers must kill the illusion that because the occupants of the inner suburbs were poor they were stupid as well. The music hall audience was cynical and anti-authoritarian, and the many songs which cut the police force down to size were warmly welcomed. The New Police Force introduced by Sir Robert Peel in 1829 soon had its commentators and when, shortly after its formation, a policeman stole a piece of mutton from a butcher's shop in Somers Town, the chorus of 'The New Policeman' was whistled all over town:

Hullo, New Police,
Who in blue coats strut on,
Your fame you won't increase
By stealing joints of mutton.

Another song was equally welcomed. Concerned with an Irishman who comes to London to join the police, the last verse goes:

I'm known to all the prigs in town—
To learned thieves well known my face is;
The frail ones, too, my favours own,
And charge me naught for sweet embraces.
And if they're going a house to rob,
Don't I watch (as is my duty?)
But never splits about the job,
For don't myself get half the booty!

Typical of the way in which topical events were immediately aired on the music hall stage was 'The Galloping Snob of Rotten Row'. A young man named Charles Southwell was riding in Rotten Row when he knocked down the aged Commissioner of Police, Sir Richard Mayne. Southwell was summoned, and fined £2 10s (£2.50), and the news item was seized upon by the song writers and by the singer Vance:

> As I go a-riding down Rotten Row, Rotten Row,
>   Rotten Row,
> The people all say, 'What a raree show!
> Oh, isn't this a go!'
> (Chorus) Riding on a cob,
>   Cantering bib-bob,
>   They say, 'There goes the snob, the snob,
>   The galloping snob of Rotten Row!'
> And once I perceived an aristocrat, 'ristocrat, 'ristocrat.
> I put my cob at him and knocked him flat,
>   All in Rotten Row.
> The bobbies they hollered out, 'Draw your rein,
> Draw your rein, draw your rein,
> And see how you've spilt Sir Richard Mayne,
>   All in Rotten Row.'

As the years went by the police acquired comic overtones, as in Lloyd's 'Policeman 92X':

> I'm the man wot takes to pris'n
> He who steals wot isn't his'n.
> X yer know is my division,
> Number ninety-two.

This attitude towards the police by the music hall audience was mirrored by the popularity of Offenbach's 'The Gendarmes' Duet' (1871), the police sergeant's song from *The Pirates of Penzance* (1880) ('When Constabulary duty's to be done/A Policeman's Lot is not a happy one'), 'Many a Time'[30] and the culmination of policemen's songs, 'If You Want to Know the Time Ask a P'liceman' (1889).

The underlying suspicion of the police, only overlaid by laughter, was seized upon by the singer Harry Randall in 1888. In 1886, Sir Charles Warren had been appointed Commissioner of Police, and received a bad press on

27 (opposite)
'My Aesthetic Love or Utterly Utter Consummate Too Too' by T. S. Lonsdale and W. G. Eaton, with a superb cover illustration dated 1881 by Concanen. This song was sung by Vance, who found that in mocking the aesthetic movement promoted by Wilde and Whistler he was at one with his audience. The aesthetes stirred up the most intense prejudices of the lower and middle classes; there was dancing in the streets when Oscar Wilde was indicted for homosexual practices. Concanen has compressed into this cover many of the elements of the movement—the passion for blue and white china, the aesthetic style of dress, the sunflower motif, the floral wallpaper, and the Arts and Crafts furniture.

28 (overleaf)
'Winning the Gloves' by J. E. Carpenter and Charles Glover, cover by R. J. Hamerton. Born in 1809, Hamerton lived through the entire history of the Victorian sheet music cover, dying in 1905, and his domestic titles have a fascinating surrealist air. Is the woman going to hit the man over the head with what looks like a 5lb weight on the table? No, she is going to persuade him to buy her a pair of white gloves. Note the urchin-like cupid at the top of the tableau.

MY ÆSTHETIC LOVE

OR UTTERLY UTTER,

CONSUMMATE TOO TOO.

WRITTEN BY

SUNG WITH IMMENSE SUCCESS BY

COMPOSED BY

T. S. LONSDALE.   THE GREAT VANCE   W. G. EATON.

She's utterly utter consummate too too!
And feeds on the lily & old china blue,
And with a sun flower she'll sit for an hour,
She's utterly utter consummate too too.

ENT. STA. HALL.

Pr. 3/

LONDON. CHARLES SHEARD, 192, HIGH HOLBORN W.C.

WINNING THE GLOVES,

COMIC BALLAD.

WRITTEN BY
J. E. CARPENTER,

COMPOSED BY
CHAS W. GLOVER.

LONDON. PUBLISHED BY B WILLIAMS 11 PATERNOSTER ROW.

"There is a tide in the affairs of men, which taken at the flood, leads on to fortune." Shakespeare.

WAIT FOR THE TURN OF THE TIDE.

"Then try to be happy and gay my boys,
Remember the world is wide,
And Rome wasn't built in a day my boys,
So wait for the turn of the tide."

WRITTEN & SUNG WITH IMMENSE SUCCESS BY

Mr HARRY CLIFTON.
AT HIS POPULAR CONCERTS.
COMPOSED BY

CHARLES COOTE JUNR

account of his heavy-handedness and brutality in quelling a demonstration by the unemployed in Trafalgar Square. The Home Secretary forced him to resign, and Randall introduced a song at the Oxford Music Hall:

Who killed Cock Warren? I said the Home Sec.,
I broke his neck; I killed Cock Warren.
And the roughs in the Square fell a-sighing and a-sobbing
When they heard of the death of poor Cock Warren.

This dislike of authority extended also to the Income Tax. In 1842 the song 'The New Income Tax' made its appearance. The masses were also sceptical about the 1840 penny post system and the song 'The Penny Post Act' voiced this. Anything new was worth commenting upon. The introduction of the omnibus created in its backwash 'The Miseries of an Omnibus', and the 1834 'Hansom Cab Song' needs no explanation for its existence.

In 1838 an Act was passed forcing cab drivers and omnibus drivers and conductors to wear a badge. A new post was needed to enforce this Act and the office of Registrar of Metropolitan Public Carriages was filled by Daniel Whittle Harvey, MP. It might be thought that this was not an Act that would arouse indignation. But all government Bills that curbed free enterprise were unwelcome, and it was felt that the 'jarvies' (a cant name for cab-drivers, 'a compliment paid to the class in consequence of one of them named Jarvis having been hanged') were having a rough deal. Sung in the role of a cab-driver, the song went:

A plague upon these meddling men, these Woods and Whittle Harveys,
For putting forth a hact like this to ruinate us jarveys.
They say we bears bad characters—it may be as they say, sirs—
But I'd ax who bears a good 'un what lives on the highway, sirs?

No topic was too sacrosanct for the music hall singer or the artists and publishers of sheet music. During the 1885 Dilke scandal, Macdermott sang 'Master Dilke Upset the Milk When Taking it Home to Chelsea'. Dilke was a politician of high promise, but he was heavily

58

29 (previous page)
'Wait for the Turn of the Tide' by Harry Clifton. This cover, depicting the composer/singer, is interesting to compare with the covers by Maguire the younger portraying the same man. This extremely fine, subtle cover is by Concanen alone, working without his associate, Lee. Clifton was very good with uplift songs, assuring his audience that things would improve:

Then try to be happy and gay my boys,
Remember the world is wide,
And Rome wasn't built in a day, my boys,
So wait for the turn of the tide.

The songs of Harry Clifton, related the Sun *newspaper in 1867, 'supply a want which has long existed, viz. a lively, merry ditty, that can be sung at a private family party, either by lady or gentleman, without the fear of offending propriety'. Although Clifton never had the charisma of Leybourne and Vance, he was an accomplished and endearing performer.*

30 (opposite)
'Many a Time' by Arthur West, cover by H. G. Banks. Banks, the successor to Concanen, favoured the use of vignettes in his covers, which detract from the over-all design but give an added pictorial interest.

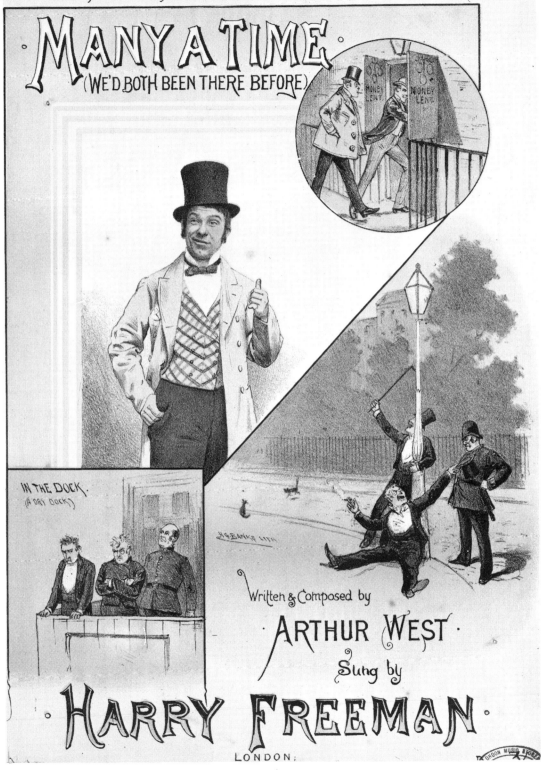

involved in what was known as the 'three in a bed' divorce case which ruined his career. The suspicion that he was framed by political opponents is neither here nor there, though Macdermott added another nail to the coffin.

Charles Parnell, 'the uncrowned king of Ireland', the one man who could have brought peace to Ireland in the nineteenth century, was ruined by his being cited by Captain O'Shea as co-respondent in an 1890 divorce. Gleefully the music hall singers added their iota of misery —'Charlie Parnell's Naughty Shape Went Stealing Down the Fire Escape'. Hard as the verdict of the mass communication medium of the nineteenth century was on their betters who overstepped the line, one cannot help admiring the pointed wit of the song writers and the unbridled innuendo of the performers, frequently one and the same person.

The Tichborne Case of 1871 was another legal highspot for music hall comment. In 1866 Arthur Orton came to England from Australia claiming to be the long-lost heir to a baronetcy and the massive Tichborne estates. The case lasted 102 days, the costs amounted to £200,000, and eventually the jury stopped the case, Orton was arrested for perjury and sentenced to fourteen years. Sir John Coleridge, later Lord Chief Justice, was the prosecutor, and his often-used phrase 'Would you be surprised to hear?' served as a song title, while references to Orton are commonplace in music hall songs of the period.

When the Shah of Persia came to Britain in 1873, Vance had a song 'Have you Seen the Shah?' When there was talk of selling Jumbo the elephant for £2,000 to the circus magnate Barnum, Macdermott made a song about that, too:

Oh, Englishmen, can it be true?
For a paltry two thousand they're going to part
With old Jumbo, the pet of the Zoo?

The introduction of the velocipede in the 1860s did not escape comment:

The Velocipedes are all the go,
In country and in town,

31 (opposite)
'The Crystal Palace Quadrille' was just one attempt to capitalise on the Great Exhibition of 1851. When the Crystal Palace was moved from Hyde Park to Sydenham, there was another opportunity.

60

THE
CRYSTAL PALACE QUADRILLE.

ENGLAND'S WELCOME TO THE NATIONS, with Portrait of Prince Albert (Song)   6 d

QUADRILLE OF ALL NATIONS, with a View of the Palace   6 d

THE PAXTON & CRYSTAL PALACE POLKAS   3 d

THE GREAT EXHIBITION POLKA & GALOP   3 d

THE GORLITZA OF ALL NATIONS   3 d

London:

G. H. DAVIDSON, 19, Peter's Hill, S! Paul's.

Nº 641-2. THE MUSICAL TREASURY.

The patent dandy, hobby-horse
  It everywhere goes down.

All forms of cycling came in for the Lions Comique treatment, culminating in the famous 'Bicycle Made for Two', and so did the craze for roller-skating in the 1870s [16]; Waldteufel's 'The Skater's Waltz' was written for the roller-skating vogue. When sixty-six balloons were released from Paris to help relieve the Prussian siege in the Franco-Prussian War, this initiated not only new music hall songs but encouraged publishers to reissue earlier balloon songs. 'Up in a Balloon' was a best seller and can still be heard, although not so often as a tune written about the exploits of the trapeze artist Léotard, who did an act at the Alhambra in the 1860s—'The Daring Young Man on the Flying Trapeze', revived as a waltz in the 1930s.

The 1862 Great Exhibition was given more coverage than the more famous one of 1851 [31], and several songs were written about it, one of the best being sung by Harry Clifton:

I went in a sixpenny omnibus
  To the Exhibition of Sixty-Two;
On a seat by the right-hand side of the door
  Sat a dark girl dressed in blue.

One of the most amusing of the *causes célèbres* of the mid-Victorian age occurred in 1875 when Colonel Valentine Baker was fined £500, imprisoned for a year and cashiered, for kissing a girl in a railway train. Almost as soon as the jury had given their verdict, 'The Kiss in the Railway Train' was being sung in the music halls.

When Chang Woo-Gow, aged nineteen, 7ft 8in, was put on show at the Westminster Aquarium in 1865, 'Chang, the Fychow Giant' was soon being sung. 'The Wreck of the London Bridge' appears to have anticipated an event that never happened. When a live gorilla was first seen in London, the songwriters were soon busy [32]. The bards of the music hall were generally sceptical about the march of Victorian technology, and preserved a sardonic tone for electricity—

Oh, have you heard the latest news of how the world's
  to be

32 (opposite)
'The Gorilla Quadrille', music by C. H. R. Marriott, cover illustration by Concanen and Lee, was written because of the vogue for gorillas. In 1861 gorilla skins and skulls were shown in London, but it was not until 1876 that a live one was seen in England. This gorilla soon died, but another was brought to London in 1879 and exhibited at the Crystal Palace. The composer Marriott always managed to get his name in the actual illustration; it is here twice, on the conductor's music and the violinist's music. Concanen always adds something to the main subject; the cameo of the flautist on the left is a gem.

62

Soon lighted up from pole to pole by electricity?

The music hall steered clear of religion, unlike the satirical papers of the day, but the movement known as spiritualism was too rich in comic possibilities to leave out, resulting in 'Knock, knock, my ma's a medium'.

Novelty being important, it is not surprising that the songwriters sometimes scraped the barrel in looking for events to commemorate[32], but when there did not seem to be anything happening in London to tickle the public, there were always general trends to fall back upon, movements that are now social historians' material. The most significant of these in the principal period of the sheet music cover was the aesthetic movement.

So far as the music hall audience was concerned, the aesthetic movement was Oscar Wilde, large, flabby, loose-lipped and soulful, and this view was also held by *Punch*, which diligently attacked 'culchah' from 1880 onwards, and Gilbert and Sullivan, whose satire on the aesthetic movement, *Patience*, appeared in 1881. Macdermott was on to the mood of the times even earlier, and 'Hildebrandt Montrose' dates from the 1870s:

His scarf, unlike himself, is green
  His gloves, 'no kid', are yeller,
His washed-out pants are well strapp'd down,
  He carries a 'fake' umbrella.
His hair is in Barber's ringlets,
  His eyes are made up dark,
He walks upon his uppers
  While strolling in the park.

The songs about the aesthetes could be even more pointed:

I'm a very Sunflowery, Aprily showery,
Eastcheapy, Towery man.
I'm a very aesthetic young man,
A non-energetic young man;
Slippity, sloppity over the shoppity,
Flippity flop young man.
I'm a bitter and mildly
Naturally childy,
Oscary Wyldy [sic] man.
I'm a Fuller's earth colour young man,
A greeny and 'Yuller' young man,

33 (opposite)
'The Showman' by C. Linda and J. Woolley has a fine characteristic cover by Concanen.

34 (overleaf)
'Moet and Chandon' by H. Hurrille and George Leybourne is of 1870 vintage, when Leybourne and Vance were vying with each other in extolling the merits of various wines. Not surprisingly there was never a shortage of champagne in the Leybourne dressing-room, while for Vance, Clicquot was 'the stuff to make you jolly'. The cover illustration of Leybourne is by Concanen.

THE SHOWMAN.

WRITTEN BY
CHAS. LINDA,

COMPOSED BY
J. WOOLLEY,

SUNG WITH THE GREATEST SUCCESS
BY
HYRAM TRAVERS.

LONDON; HOPWOOD & CREW, 42, NEW BOND ST w.

R 3/-

MOET AND CHANDON.

ALL RIGHTS RESERVED & ENT? STA? HALL.
ACCORDING TO ACT OF PARL?!

CONCANEN, LITH.

STANNARD & SON, 7, POLAND S?

WRITTEN BY
H. HURRILLE,
COMPOSED, & SUNG WITH THE GREATEST SUCCESS
BY
GEORGE LEYBOURNE.

LONDON: HOPWOOD & CREW, 42, NEW BOND ST? W.

Pr 3/-

CLICQUOT,

ALL RIGHTS RESERVED & ENT.D STA.S HALL,
FEB.Y 5.TH 1870, ACCORDING TO ACT OF PARL.NT

"Clicquot! Clicquot! that's the stuff to make you jolly,
Clicquot! Clicquot! Soon will banish melancholy,
Clicquot! Clicquot! Drinking other wine is folly,
Clicquot! Clicquot! That's the drink for me."

WRITTEN BY
FRANK W. GREEN,
COMPOSED BY
J. RIVIERE,

SUNG WITH IMMENSE SUCCESS
BY

THE GREAT VANCE.

LONDON.
HOPWOOD & CREW, 42, NEW BOND STREET.

Pr 3/-

STANNARD & SON. IMP.

Pretty externally 'Patience' and 'Colonely'
Utterly utter young man.

This is an exceptionally interesting song, for it indicates
how well specialised references were understood by the
music hall audience. The reference to *Patience* is obvious,
but the more obscure mention of 'Colonely' could only
make sense to a listener aware that in the play *The Colonel*
by F. C. Burnand, Wilde appears as Lambert Streyke.

Also indicative of this hostile mood towards 'outsiders'
was the song 'My Aesthetic Love'[27], the cover of which
was illustrated by Concanen. Not only do these songs
confirm the music hall audience's interest in things
happening outside their own preserves; they also indicate
the suspicion of anything that they did not understand.
The aesthetes might have been men on the moon for all
they knew.

Yet the same kind of sartorial inventiveness was present
in their own ranks. The costermongers were celebrated
for the way in which they dressed up on Sundays, bud-
ding Pearly Kings (see the cover to 'The Showman'[33]),
and the extravagances of the Lions Comique needed no
pointing. As swells and mashers, Leybourne and the rest
gloried in the peculiar modes of dress that they
adopted[34][35]. The difference was that the Lion Comique
was one of them. He could be identified with, even when
he mocked them, as Vance did in this bit of spoken
business between the verses of his songs:

Yaas, the drinking habits of the populace are simply
disgusting. What the deuce do they want with beer in
the middle of the day? They're not up all night at balls
and parties, and they don't get jolly in the small
hours. . . .

The audience loved it, they loved the way in which
Leybourne and Macdermott went from hall to hall in
their carriages drawn by four white horses (all provided
by the management), and they loved to be mocked. The
men in the audience were swells by proxy. For a time
they could escape from their humdrum environment.
But of course the Lions were not like them; they were
shrewd professionals, giving the audience what they
wanted, encouraging them to identify.

68

35 (previous page)
*'Clicquot' by Frank Green and J.
Riviere is another 1870 song of the
wine war between Vance and Leybourne. A splendid cover by Concanen
showing the 'Great' Vance in all his
glory—top hat, monocle, cane, kid
gloves and fur-collared jacket.*

36 (opposite)
*'I'm a Ship Without a Rudder' by
Frank Vernon and Harry Hunter,
cover by Concanen. A marvellous
portrayal of foolish gull and saucy
minx. The theme of the jilted man is
common in music hall song, and
Concanen has caught the mixture of
comedy and pathos with unerring skill.*

HARRY HUNTER'S NEW SONG.

I'M A SHIP WITHOUT A RUDDER.

CHORUS. "I'm a ship without a rudder, I'm a bird without a wing,
I'm a girl without a chignon, I'm a wasp without a sting,
I'm a tree without a leaf, I'm a jail without a thief,
Since Lucy left me all alone in misery & grief."

COMPOSED BY

FRANK VERNON,

WRITTEN & SUNG BY

HARRY HUNTER.

ENT. STA. HALL.   PRICE 3/-

LONDON; HOPWOOD & CREW, 42, NEW BOND St W.

Their domestic songs are equally attuned to the life style of their admirers. The love songs are wry, with a tendency towards the cruel[36], and a tale of mishaps is often wittily unfolded[37]. For the working classes and the lower middle classes which made up the bulk of these admirers, courtship was a brief respite in the daily grind, and in dealing with this state the singers have a light delicate touch that is more effective because it is so rare:

The artful little fishes have a sly and roguish look,
And seem to wink at couples flirting in some shady
   nook,
What funny stories they could tell, if they but had the
   knack,
Of hearts and smarts and Cupid's darts that fly around
   the 'Aq'.

The Aq, of course, is our old friend Westminster Aquarium.

Courtship was succinctly summed up in:
Something rather dangerous, something rather nice,
Something rather naughty, though it can't be called
   a vice,
Many say it's nonsense, others think it wrong,
All agree it's jolly, though it don't last long.

Yet even courtship could have its trials and tribulations, as we can see in the following spoken business by Vance. The girl has only one leg ('Her leg comes down with a dot and carry one, As she stumps along so gaily').

'Shake a leg!' I thought I should have expired when mother mentioned it. Father said, 'Put your best leg foremost; get married, and put your legs under your own mahogany.' Legs! Three between the two of us— a matrimonial tripod. . . .

Unrequited love was apt to be amusing rather than heart-rending:

Nancy fancied a soldier, Nancy fancied a snob,
Nancy fancied a nobleman who wasn't worth a bob.
Nancy fancied a sailor who's sailing on the sea,
She fancied a slop with a carroty mop, but never could
   fancy me.

Or:

I feel like beef without mustard,

37 (opposite)
'Two in the Morning', a nicely executed monochrome cover by Alfred Concanen.

70

Or a woman that's had a divorce,
I feel like a crab on a fishmonger's slab,
Or a cove who his senses has lost.
I feel like tea without sugar,
Or very bad fourpenny ale,
For the loss of Jemima, my foolish Jemima,
Who after the Prince did sail.

Married life according to the music hall singers was coping with screaming babies, bullying slatternly wives and searching for accommodation. There was nothing to hold the audience quite like being specific about small things (see the detail of [33]). A London audience appreciated local references, such as those contained in the following song, delivered by James Fawn:

We first lived in Clapham, and then went to Chatham,
From Chatham we moved up to Oxford Street West;
And then the next quarter we spent in Bayswater,
But there, don't you know, 'twas like all the rest.
We've had rooms called attics, and had rheumatics,
And down in the kitchen we've pall'd with the cats;
And had such nice diggings in Peabody's Buildings,
Then lived you must know for three weeks in flats.

The great ability of the music hall stars to change their personae to suit the song was very important. It was unthinkable for the swell and masher to be domesticated. When we come to uplift songs, then the switch from mindless swell to stern patriot was a feat of some magnitude. The best singers could do it, and played on their audience as if on a many-stringed instrument. The individuals were welded into a mob, and when Macdermott sang 'We Don't Want to Fight, But by Jingo If We Do' in 1878 at the time of the Russo-Turkish War there is not much doubt that had he asked the audience to follow him into battle to save the poor little Turk they would have done this *en masse*.

After this success, Macdermott was known as 'the Statesman of the Halls', and it was rumoured that the song was subsidised by the Conservative Party, just as Leybourne's 'Champagne Charlie' was subsidised by the champagne shippers to the extent of £20 a week.

'Very potent, cheap music', said a character in Nöel

38 (opposite)
'Oh Lor, Oh Lor! Oh Dear, Oh Dear!' by Frank Green, Oswald Allan and Edmund Forman, cover by Concanen, a superb evocation of the age. This was what the Victorian interior was really like. From glass rolling pin on the wall to fairground ornaments on the mantelpiece, Concanen does not put a foot wrong. Beneath the signature there are two letters, 'H.A.'. Between 1881 and 1885 Concanen used a date code on his covers: H.A.= 1881, H.B.=1882, H.C.=1883, H.D.=1884, H.E.=1885.

WRITTEN EXPRESSLY FOR THE COMING PANTOMIMES.

OH LOR, OH LOR! OH DEAR, OH DEAR!

A CYNICAL SONG BY

FRANK W. GREEN & OSWALD ALLAN.

MUSIC BY

EDMUND FORMAN.

LONDON: FRANCIS BROS & DAY, (BLENHEIM HOUSE,) 195, OXFORD ST W.

Pr 3/

Coward's *Private Lives*, and despite their hard crust the music hall audience could be got at by appeals to their patriotism and their finer qualities, being surprised by their own genuine sorrow at the death of Gladstone when it was artfully played upon. The temperance movement produced its own bards, and the last phrase of one song can sum up this genre—'My father's a drunkard, my mother is dead'.

In its reaction to tear-jerkers, the working class audience was at one with its betters. 'I shall never forget Grisi's rendering of "The Minstrel Boy" at the Crystal Palace', wrote Mrs E. M. Ward, the artist. 'She refused to sing again after three encores. The audience who had listened to her singing spellbound, rose in a mass, and the applause was like thunder. It seemed as if the glass roof would shatter, it was so tremendous.' Similarly Charles Godfrey's 'On the Bridge at Midnight' tugged on the heart-strings.

The uplift songs inculcate such qualities as playing the game, comradeship, and class solidarity. This sort of song was particularly popular in the 1850s and 1860s, with 'There's a Good Time Coming', 'Brighter Days Will Come'[39], 'Let's Enjoy Life While We Can'[40] and 'Wait for the Turn of the Tide'[29], conning the audience into the belief that things were getting better (they were not—there was great unemployment in the 1860s). The Lions Comique did this type of song with tongue in cheek, with slight pauses and 'ers' and 'ums' to indicate that they knew that the listeners were too sophisticated to be taken in by this claptrap.

The writers of music hall songs were a mixed crew. By and large they were ill-paid for their work, G. W. Hunt getting 1 guinea (£1.05) for 'We Don't Want to Fight', Henry Pettitt half a guinea for 'If Ever There was a Damned Scamp', while Fred Gilbert got £10 for 'The Man Who Broke the Bank at Monte Carlo', based on the career of Charles Wells who did break the bank, six times. Charles Coborn, the singer, made £600 in royalties.

The writers dealt directly with the music hall singers, and unquestionably had a raw deal, especially when one

39 (opposite)
'Brighter Days Will Come' by Leigh Wilson, cover by Richard Childs. Childs was a prolific and uneven artist, given to drink, and in this cover he seems to have been affected by the unmitigated gloom of the song, in which it is plain that brighter days aren't coming.

74

BRIGHTER DAYS
WILL COME

CHILDS & HARRIS Delt. et. Lith.

WRITTEN & COMPOSED BY

LEIGH WILSON

ENT. STA. HALL,

Pr 3/-

LONDON

SINCLAIR & Cº 40. Cᵀ MARLBOROUGH Sᵀ

Bristol,

W.J WORBOYES, IMP GREEK Sᵀ W.

PHILIP J. SMITH & SONS, PIANO FORTE MAKERS.

considers the high quality of some of their lyrics which compare favourably with the light verse being written by fashionable poets of the time. It will be apparent that there are some extremely witty turns of phrase, some subtle punning, and evidence of high intelligence in the use of contemporary slang and language. Indeed, some of these phrases have found a niche in common usage.

Many of the songs were written by the singers, Vance, Leybourne and Macdermott claiming authorship of numbers of their successes. In the early days of the saloon, tavern concert, and cider cellar, the singers hawked their songs about the tables without loss of prestige.

When we turn to the music, then we must confess that most of it is sad stuff, unless a catchy tune is automatically good. In many cases the quadrilles and polkas of the 1840s and 1850s were merely rigged out with words, but this did not matter, for delivery and content were all.

So many different music hall songs were coming off the press that it was not possible to compose sufficiently differentiated tunes for specific songs. The repertoire of folk song was looted, and Handel's 'Halleluiah Chorus' and 'La Donne e Mobile' served for 'Yes, We Have No Bananas' and 'Ta-ra-ra-boom-de-ay'. The quantity of Victorian music hall tunes that are still in the repertoire does not alter the fact that 95 per cent of the music was disposable, and in recognising that music hall tunes are part of the aural environment, one must not forget the large part that nostalgia and childhood recollection play.

But why should they be any better than they are? They are certainly no worse than their equivalent in 'serious' Victorian music, the drawing-room ballad, and it is interesting to remember that the master of the rum-ti-tum tune, Sir Arthur Sullivan, was also the composer of 'The Lost Chord'.

Music hall tunes can be seen as the forerunner of piped music. The latter sells food in supermarkets and contributes to a happy atmosphere in factories, offices and aircraft terminals. The former also made for a happy atmosphere, and they sold the words of a song; a good tune might divert attention away from the singer, and this would never have done.

40 (opposite)
'Let's Enjoy Life While We Can' by Charles Merion, cover by W. R. Mallyon. The somewhat grumpy expression of Miss Annie Adams the singer is at odds with the sentiments of the chorus.

> *Come along and join my song, and let's all sing,*
> *While to aid the merry strain your glasses ring,*
> *Come along and join my song, and let's all sing,*
> *While to aid the merry strain your glasses ring.*

Although Mallyon, born in 1840, was associated with Concanen in the printing firm of Stannard & Dixon, little of the verve and vitality has rubbed off on him. This single-colour cover is sober and sensitive.

LETS ENJOY LIFE WHILE WE CAN.

SUNG BY

MISS ANNIE ADAMS.

ENT, STA, HALL.

PRICE. 2/6

LONDON;
G. EMERY & Cº 408, OXFORD STREET, W.

4 THE ARTISTS

The greatest name in the execution of pictorial sheet music covers is Alfred Concanen. He and John Brandard are the only specialists in this field to be systematically collected, and it is from their surviving work that one gets an idea of the quantity of sheet music that was published. No estimate of the number of covers that Concanen did can be more than an approximation, but at least 400 titles have been traced.

Alfred Concanen, son of an artist and of Irish descent, was born in London in 1835. Concanen was a man of slight build with a blond moustache, something of a dandy, good-hearted, generous, a pale copy of the Lions Comique whom he immortalised on the lithographic stone. In 1858 he was married at a London registry office, his address being given as 43 Bloomsbury Street, and this same year he began work in earnest as a music cover illustrator, occupying studios in Frith Street that he retained during most of his working life.

Biographical details of Concanen and the other music cover artists are sparse, but we do know that Concanen's activities were not restricted to music covers. In 1869 he illustrated *Carols of Cockayne* by H. S. Leigh; in 1874 he illustrated *The Wilds of London* by James Greenwood, a raffish probing journalist of the Charles Dickens mould, and in 1876 *Low Life Deeps* by the same author. He also designed posters[41]. Concanen died in 1886; Gordon Craig, the theatrical designer, claimed that he, then a boy of sixteen, met Concanen in a pub near the Strand on the night that he died.

For a time Concanen was a staff illustrator for the *Illustrated Sporting and Dramatic News*, and here he unquestionably got into the habit of working from photographs. Although photography was by then a sophisticated art, no commercial method had been found of printing photographs in newspapers and periodicals; the steel engraving such as [42] and the woodcut still ruled the roost. Photographs were starting-off points, and it was

41 (opposite)
'Cox and Box', words by F. C. Burnand, music by Arthur Sullivan. Concanen was not only a prolific artist in the music cover field; he illustrated books specialising in raffish London subjects, and executed posters as in this example. Lithography was the perfect medium for large designs. This lively piece dates from 1869.

78

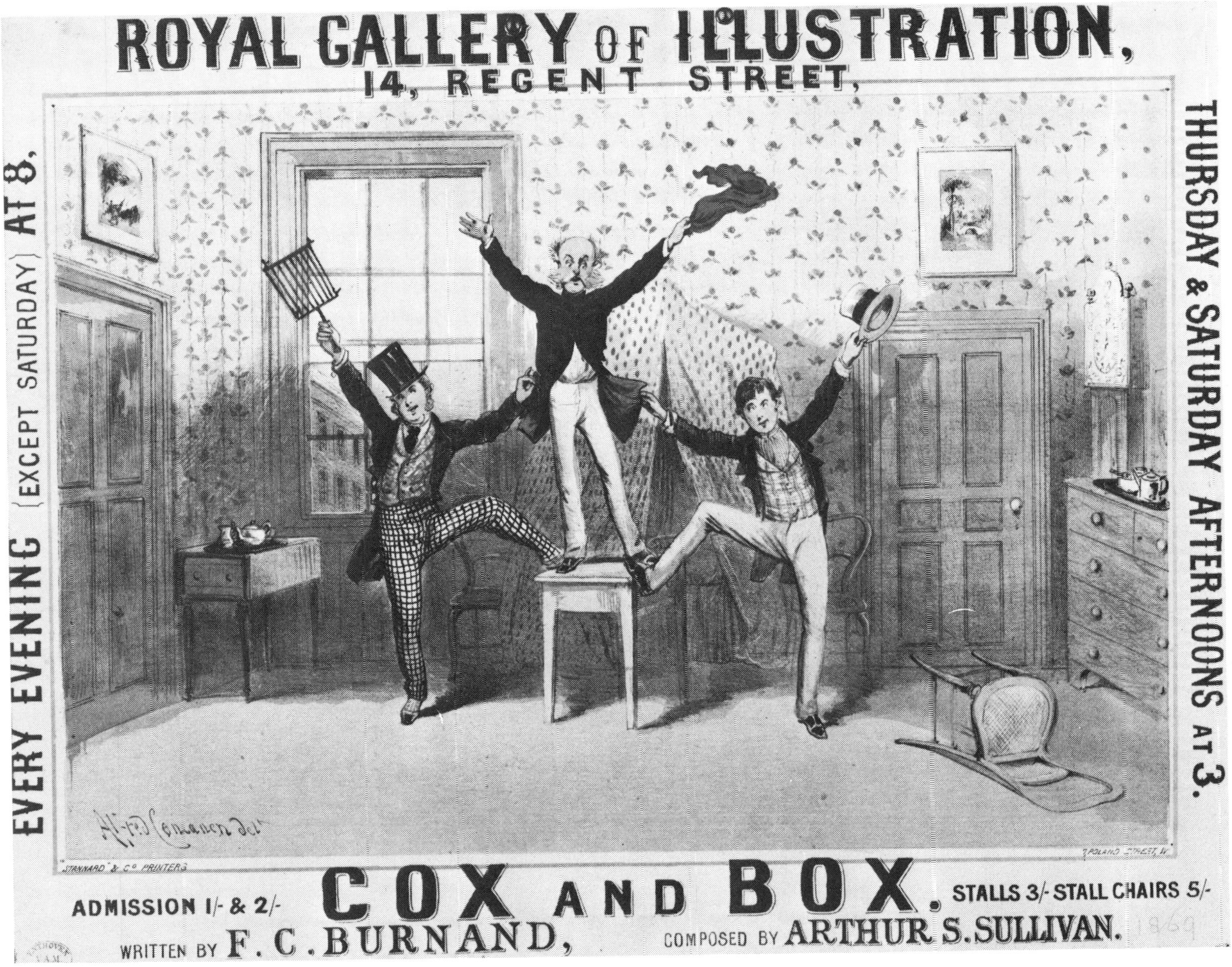
ROYAL GALLERY OF ILLUSTRATION,
14, REGENT STREET,
EVERY EVENING (EXCEPT SATURDAY) AT 8,
THURSDAY & SATURDAY AFTERNOONS AT 3.
STANNARD & Co PRINTERS
7 POLAND STREET, W.
COX AND BOX.
ADMISSION 1/- & 2/-
STALLS 3/- STALL CHAIRS 5/-
WRITTEN BY F. C. BURNAND,
COMPOSED BY ARTHUR S. SULLIVAN.
1869

considered all right to use them as artists' aids. An example of high art using photographs is Frith's *Derby Day* (1858).

Concanen worked in close association with an artist named Lee, and frequently the two names appear on music covers. Concanen was always the major partner, Lee being responsible for letter work, 'ornamentals', and accessories[43] and [44]. The bravura, the sweep of the design, the composition, the colouring, were all Concanen's.

His work falls broadly into two parts—straightforward portraits of the music hall singers in costume as in [45], finely executed and as bright as a new pin, and genre scenes illustrating the title. 'The Excursion Train' depicts a platform scene on Victoria Station, a confusion of day-trippers clambering into the Brighton train[17]; 'The Flunkey or She Loved a Man With a Monkey' portrays a top-hatted servant in collision with an organ-grinder and his monkey; 'Ain't You Sorry You Dress'd Yourself' shows a disgruntled swell with a dirty footprint on his white waistcoat caused by an urchin doing handsprings on the pavement; 'The Husband's Boat' centres around a bucolic bunch of trippers on board a paddle-steamer to Margate.

Knife-board omnibuses, costermongers' barrows, carriages and hackney cabs, the hustle and bustle of London life, these are frozen on to the lithographic stone by Concanen[46]. London out-of-doors is his special interest; he did not much care for domestic scenes, leaving these to other illustrators.

Not unnaturally, considering the volume of work he turned out, Concanen's work is uneven, but he never pot-boiled as some of his colleagues did. It is surprising that in the endless series of illustrations of music hall singers in costume he never falls below a certain level. The quality of the stone seems to have stimulated Concanen, who did not need new-fangled substitutes such as prepared zinc.

Although Concanen is the master of the lithographed music cover, it must not be supposed that other artists in this sphere are of little interest. In straight portraiture Henry Maguire the younger is as proficient, and in

42 (opposite)

'The Roman Fall' by Alfred Lee, cover by Concanen, is dated 1870. It thus belongs to the best period of the music cover and is a magnificent example of the artistry of Concanen in depicting the period swell. This is the kind of song Vance, the cover figure, did so well:

> *The Grecian Bend for West-end Belles,*
> *Is thought by Jove the thing,*
> *The Roman Fall for Pall Mall Swells,*
> *Is what my boys I sing;*
> *Heads up, chests out la militaire,*
> *How graceful the effect,*
> *How stylish yet how debonnaire (sic),*
> *It is the walk correct.*

THE ROMAN FALL,

ALL RIGHTS RESERVED & ENT^D STA^S HALL.
JAN^Y 26TH 1870, ACCORDING TO ACT OF PARL^{MT}

"The Roman Fall, the Roman Fall,
That graceful arch the Roman Fall,
The wonder of the age I call,
The Swell's own walk, The Roman Fall."

A CONCANEN, DEL & LITH.

WRITTEN BY | COMPOSED BY
HUGH WILLOUGHBY SWENY ESQ^{RE} | ALFRED LEE,
SUNG WITH IMMENSE SUCCESS
BY
VANCE,
AT HIS
POPULAR CONCERTS IN LONDON AND THE PROVINCES.

P_R 3/-

LONDON: HOPWOOD & CREW, 42, NEW BOND STREET, W.

domestic vignettes R. J. Hamerton must be highly reckoned.

Artists concerned with the sheet music cover can be divided roughly into two classes: artists and illustrators. Although the nineteenth century was very kind to artists, and men such as Rossetti could command thousands of pounds for water-colours, there were those who were forced to think commercially to make a living. Executing sheet music covers was to them a poor substitute for easel paintings. This can sometimes be seen when artists of this kind do an equivalent of an easel painting for a specific cover, ignoring the theme of the song or at best using it as a taking-off point.

John Brandard was particularly prone to this. One suspects that he had a stock of orthodox landscape lithographs which he used when the title of the song was reasonably ambiguous or unspecific. A good example of a traditional artist using sheet music covers to provide bread and butter is furnished by Alexandre Laby. Born. in Calais in 1814, Laby was basically a painter of religious subjects who found some kind of fulfilment in designing covers for music on sacred and mawkish subjects (see [47]). His nearest approach to frivolity is his 'Alliance Polka' written to commemorate the rapport between Napoleon III and Queen Victoria. Although he did not die until 1899, Laby's most prolific period was in the 1850s. His main venture into Victorian high art is represented by three massive oil paintings in the church of St Joseph's Retreat, Highgate Hill. One of them depicts the death of Joseph. The combination of melancholy and sentiment in Tennyson's verse appealed very much to Laby. Composers of drawing-room ballads drew strongly on this fount, and they could rely on Laby providing suitable covers.

Another artist who found his way into music cover illustration through financial necessity rather than choice was S. Rosenthal, the quality of whose work is evident from the plate [48]. John Ruskin employed Rosenthal to lithograph his drawings for his book *Stones of Venice* (1851). Fastidious and demanding, Ruskin always used the best men available to transcribe his own pencil

43 (*opposite*)
'Little Jack Frost Quadrilles' by Arthur Henry Brown, cover by Concanen and Lee. A successful venture into fantasy by Concanen, with a most beautifully executed winter background and ingenious use of holly leaves to frame the picture.

LITTLE JACK FROST QUADRILLES,

BY

ARTHUR HENRY BROWN.

LONDON B WILLIAMS 11 PATERNOSTER ROW

drawings. Typical of Rosenthal's work were 'Auld Lang Syne Quadrille' and 'The Postman's Knock' (1855).

Maxim Gauci, born in Rome in 1774, arrived in London in 1815 after a career as a miniature painter in Paris, and found a niche in the music cover business doing such covers as 'Buy a Broom' and 'Oysters, Sir'. He died in 1854, thus missing the music hall boom. His covers were bright and competent, without quite achieving the elegance of Brandard. Richard Childs[39] was a prolific worker, doing the bulk of his work in the 1860s and 1870s. It is tempting to dismiss Childs on the evidence of some of his more clumsy covers, but at his best he has a kind of bravura and brilliance, and had he not been an alcoholic he may well have made a name in serious art.

Another interesting artist is Augustus Butler[49] who specialised in military covers. He worked for the lithographic printing firm of Stannard & Dixon in Poland Street, and when a cholera epidemic hit London and the rest of the firm fled, Butler remained behind, working. As a pure illustrator he is best known for his battle scenes from the Crimean War. T. H. Jones, who flourished around the 1840s, is of more interest in his variety of media than his variety of talent, venturing into etchings, woodcuts, lithographs, and zincographs. Many thought that zinc would replace stone for lithography, but although the surface of zinc was more reliable, most artists preferred to stick to stone.

There were some music cover artists who arrived there almost by accident. William Michael Watson was born in Newcastle in 1840 and studied music under his father; he considered himself as much a composer of songs as a music cover illustrator. His song 'Abandoned' was succeeded, appropriately enough, by 'Afloat'. Although he is little known as a music cover artist, he did some excellent work in the Concanen genre, dying in 1889.

G. E. Madeley practised sheet music cover illustration mainly because he was the owner of a printing firm. He specialised in Nigger Minstrel songs, a form of entertainment that dates from the 1830s. Far more important both as illustrators and printers were the Leighton Brothers[50];

44 (opposite)
'After Dark' by Charles Coote, junior, cover by Concanen. Concanen was strong on railway trains and this melodramatic cover is one of his best. Three colours only—black, white and red (with its allied quarter and half tints).

DEDICATED TO TOM ROBERTS ESQRE

AFTER DARK,
GALOP.

INTRODUCING THE CELEBRATED SONG OF **TOMMY DODD**, AS SUNG WITH GREAT APPLAUSE IN **AFTER DARK**.
BY PERMISSION OF **DION BOUCICAULT ESQRE**
COMPOSED BY

CHARLES COOTE, JUNR.

ENT. STA. HALL.

London, HOPWOOD & CREW, 42, New Bond St. W.

PRICE
DUETT
SEPTETT

ALFRED CONCANEN LITH

STANNARD & SON IMP

they are especially interesting in that they used the Baxter system of printing in oil colours, polychromatic printing, in which 'every degree of evanescence in the outline can be obtained; and 50,000 facsimiles of a painting may be produced with perfect uniformity and at a moderate expense'.

Charles Blair Leighton studied under the historical painter, B. R. Haydon, and designed a number of music covers in the 1840s. Born in 1823, Charles Leighton died young, in 1855. His brother George studied under George Baxter (1804–67) and utilised this knowledge of oil colour printing in the business, but although an artist of ability, George Leighton was mainly concerned with administration, printing, and the publishing of *The Illustrated London News*.

But the above are minor figures compared with Concanen, Brandard, and three other artists, Henry Maguire[12] and [13], Walter Robert Mallyon[40] and Robert Jacob Hamerton[28]. There were three Maguires in the music cover business, Henry the elder, Henry the younger, and T. H. Maguire. Of these Henry the younger is by far the most important. Henry the elder was more interested in the fine arts, and illustrated the Gothic revival work of Pugin. He is of the polka and quadrille brigade of the Jullien/Brandard era, and it is only necessary to mention two of his works, 'Real Scotch Polkas' of 1844 and 'Polish Mazourkas' of 1845. Henry the younger was an all-round professional, and like Concanen he was very prolific. His portraiture was exceptionally good, and although he perhaps lacks the bite and incisiveness of Concanen, his genre pieces, such as 'Up in a Balloon' for Leybourne in 1868, are extremely competent.

Many of his covers were for music hall songs written for Arthur Lloyd, and he was very strong in uplift songs such as 'Act on the Square', 'Just to Show There's No Ill Feeling' and 'Wheel of Life'. Despite this propensity, his interests went down rather than up—woodcuts for the *London Journal*, and gruesome potboilers for cheap boys' fiction with titles like *Broad Arrow Jack* and *Alone in the Pirate's Lair*. Maguire worked with Concanen for a time, as did Mallyon.

45 (opposite)
'Dundreary's Brother Sam' by J. E. Carpenter, cover by Concanen and Lee. In 1858, Tom Taylor brought out a play Our American Cousin *in which one of the characters was Lord Dundreary, played by Edward Sothern. This character caught on in Britain to an amazing extent; Dundreary whiskers, a kind of mutton-chop beard, became famous, and it was only to be expected that Dundreary would be made the centre piece of a saga. The play in which Dundreary's brother Sam appeared was put on at the Haymarket Theatre in 1865. This classic cover is executed in Concanen's most meticulous style, and is valuable. Note that the publishers of this music managed to get their name on the musical instrument display behind brother Sam.*

86

DUNDREARY'S BROTHER SAM

"THERE OFTEN IN A PERFECT SEA, | THEY SAID, "THOSE WHISKERS" THAT MUST BE,
OF CRINOLINES I SWAM, | DUNDREARY'S BROTHER SAM.

COMIC SONG
BY
J. E. CARPENTER.

LONDON, METZLER & Cº 37, 38 & 35 Gᵀ MARLBOROUGH STREET W.
PIANOFORTE & HARMONIUM WAREROOMS, AT Nº 16.

Born in 1840, Mallyon was apprenticed to a portrait artist George Black in 1856, where he met Thomas Lee. Though he did do admirable work on his own[18], Lee worked closely with Concanen, and his name appears frequently in alliance with his, and through Lee, Mallyon was introduced to Concanen. Mallyon was clearly influenced by Concanen; at his best his work is sober, meticulous and precise, and he seems to have preferred to work in single-colour lithography.

Born in 1809, R. J. Hamerton was the longest lived of the entire fraternity of music cover illustrators, dying in 1905. He started his life as a comic draughtsman, contributing to *Punch* in 1843, and he realised the implications of lithography at an early stage. He flourished during the vogue for quadrilles and polkas in the 1840s and the music hall song period of the 1860s and later. At the age of eighty-eight Hamerton was sufficiently adventurous to try his hand at oil painting.

The distinction between artists and illustrators is that the latter group kept their text and their commission in mind, aware that they were supplementary. They did not produce irrelevancies, as Laby and Brandard could do. During the nineteenth century the use of illustration in books of every kind greatly increased, and a victim of the unprecedented demand for books backed by pictures saw the decline of copper-plate engraving, which was too costly for a cheap run of books and wore out quickly.

About 1823 copper-plate engraving was replaced by steel engraving. The effect of steel engraving was somewhat cold and hard, but it was a cheap general purpose medium and was much used by the publishers and printers of volumes of poetry, keepsakes and annuals which enjoyed a vogue. Steel engraving provided employment for large numbers of illustrators working to a formula, and the basic insensitivity of the medium was not seen when the engravings measured perhaps three or four square inches.

Hack publishers of sheet music found that steel engraving served their purpose, but the better quality line work was done on wood. This might seem anachronistic, for engraving on wood is too readily associated with the

46 (opposite)
'Mind the Paint' by N. G. Travers, cover by Concanen, a lively genre piece in green, red, black and white on a buff ground. The restraint of Concanen's palette, that could have been well-emulated by high art painters, is shown by green solely being used for the paint on the man's coat.

47 (overleaf)
'Early Love Valse' by Frank Musgrave, cover by Alexandre Laby, a religious high art painter with a propensity for mawkish subjects. Although Laby lived from 1814 to 1899, his most prolific period was in the 1850s.

88

MIND THE PAINT.

WRITTEN & COMPOSED BY
N · G · TRAVERS,
AND SUNG WITH GREAT SUCCESS BY
G. H. MACDERMOTT

"EARLY LOVE" VALSE,

DEDICATED TO

Miss Ada Swanborough.

BY

FRANK MUSGRAVE.

ENT, STA, HALL,

Solo.	4/-
Duett.	4/-
Septett.	2/-
Full Orchestra	3/6

LONDON;
METZLER & Cº 35,36,37 & 38. GREAT MARLBOROUGH STREET .W.
PIANO FORTE & HARMONIUM WAREROOMS, AT Nº 16.

THE
GIPSY QUADRILLES.

O. ROSENTHAL LITH.   7. RED LION SQUARE.

STEPHEN GLOVER.

LONDON
ROBERT COCKS & Cº, NEW BURLINGTON STREET,
by special Appointment

Nº
ENT STA HALL
COPYRIGHT

PIANO SOLO 3
DUET 4
DANCE BAND 6

name of Bewick and his followers and clumsy, naive and charming vignettes of birds and beasts. However, there had been a change of technique from the white-line method employed by Bewick to black-line illustration, drawn by the artist, cut by trade engravers, such as the Dalziel brothers.

In 1832 Charles Knight began his *Penny Magazine*, using woodcuts on a large scale. Woodcuts for 305 issues cost him £12,000. It was found that woodcuts could be stereotyped, that a matrix could be made from the original using papier-mâché, and so copies of the same illustration could be printed on more than one machine at a time. If a wood block was badly damaged there was a replica to take its place.

From 1840 onwards, the weekly press used woodcuts extensively, and in 1842 the *Illustrated London News* was first published with thirty-two woodcuts. The wide demand for graphic artists meant that talented men had no longer to cultivate the picture-buying middle and upper classes, or eke out a precarious living engraving fashionable paintings for the less wealthy. More important still than the arrival of the weekly illustrated news periodical was the appearance of *Punch*.

Punch provided a stamping ground for many illustrators involved in sheet music covers, such as Hamerton who did work for *Punch* soon after its introduction in 1841, and also influenced the styles of comic draughtsmen. There is a definite family look about the humorous engraving of the 1840s, and illustrators such as 'Phiz' (Hablot K. Browne) and Cruikshank had a great influence on the work of Alfred Ashley, a prolific producer of sheet music covers during this period ((10) and (11)).

This was a time when the saloons and taverns were in operation, the music hall having not yet arrived on the scene, and the song repertoire revolved around comic songs and heavy melodrama. One of the key figures in the saloon and tavern was Henry Russell (born 1812), famous for moral ballads such as 'Woodman, Spare that Tree' and 'The Gambler's Wife', and Ashley illustrated these, as well as music covers concerning titles from

48 (previous page)
'The Gipsy Quadrilles' by Stephen Glover, cover by S. Rosenthal, dates from the 1850s and is a splendid example of the versatility of chromolithography. It is impossible to say how many lithograph stones were used in this cover, so many and varied are the hues. Rosenthal was not only the illustrator but the printer, and was held in such high regard by Ruskin that he was entrusted with the lithographing of Ruskin's own drawings for his book Stones of Venice (1851). *It is interesting to note that eight different type faces are used on this cover without clashing.*

49 (opposite)
'The Charge of the Light Brigade' by John Blockley. Although unsigned, this lively atmospheric cover may be attributable to Augustus Butler, a specialist in military covers. Tennyson wrote the poem in 1855 during the course of the Crimean War, and Blockley seized on the opportunity to set it to music and publish it himself for a double market—the music hall whose audiences would always rise to a patriotic ditty, and the drawing-room. That he had some doubts is evident by a note half way through the music: 'This Verse may be omitted if considered too long.'

THE CHARGE OF THE LIGHT BRIGADE,

BALACLAVA

Half a league, half a league,   Cannon to right of them,
Half a league onwards;   Cannon to left of them,
All in the valley of Death   Cannon in front of them
Rode the six hundred   Volley'd & thunder'd

WRITTEN BY   COMPOSED BY

ALFRED TENNYSON ESQ.   JOHN BLOCKLEY.

MAY BE SUNG IN PUBLIC WITHOUT PERMISSION OR PAYMENT OF FEE

Dickens—'The Chimes Quadrille', 'The Cricket on the Hearth Quadrille', and 'The Cricket Polka'. This further strengthens the link with 'Phiz', best known today for his illustrations to Dickens.

The engravings by Ashley are interesting historically and pictorially. They belong to a series called the Musical Bouquet; the individual numbers were printed in quantity, which meant that copper-plate engraving, only suited to relatively short runs, was out. They were also done on the cheap, which meant that the art work was skimped. The borders of 'The Maniac'[11] are executed very incompetently, and the wall and arch on the left are completely out of perspective. On the other hand the figure in the bed and the weird faces in the gloom have an intensity that matches the mood of the song. 'The Celebrated Elfin Waltzes'[10] is a much more accomplished piece of work, and the element of the grotesque is reminiscent of another *Punch* influence, Dicky Doyle.

Although few would claim that Ashley is anything other than a relatively minor graphic artist, it is clear that he is adhering to the principles of a good illustrator; he is augmenting the interest of the subject rather than producing an illustration standing in its own right.

At this stage, the pictorial music cover was on sufferance. The music starts half-way down the sheet. The publishers have not yet realised that the cover can itself be a selling point, and that it was well worth while spending as much money on the cover as on the musical contents—or more.

The book, print and music trades, all popular, all proliferating at an amazing rate, were able to support an army of illustrators. There was no difficulty for accomplished graphic artists in getting work. Methods were streamlined. In the weekly illustrated journals, where a deadline had to be met, the large cuts were divided between several engravers, each doing their share towards the finished design, the various fragments then being reassembled and bolted together, with the joins smoothed away.

The demands of illustrated journalism made for professionalism—rapidity and skill in execution, and the

50 (opposite)
'The Star of the Night' by Charles d'Albert dates from 1853, and the high cost of this particular piece of sheet music was perhaps warranted by the process used in the illustration—oil-colour printing. Baxter prints now obtain high prices in the auction room, and the process was used fairly frequently in sheet music cover illustration, especially by the Leighton Brothers, George Leighton having studied under Baxter. This cover is unsigned but its high quality is evident; not quite good enough for Baxter himself, though, for the colour registration is not perfect.

VALSE À DEUX TEMPS,

BY

CHARLES D' ALBERT.

maximum use made of modern innovations. The best of the music cover illustrators had this kind of experience. Mention has been made of Concanen's association with periodicals, especially the *Illustrated Sporting and Dramatic News*, and his use of photographs. Another refugee from illustrated journals was Alfred Bryan, who signed his music covers with his initials. He, too, worked for the *Illustrated Sporting and Dramatic News*, as well as the *Hornet*, a short-lived satirical journal, and, briefly, *Punch*.

Training in journalism gave many music cover artists the sense of immediacy and topicality. This was important for songs that had a here and now appeal, such as those that were written around a specific event. The best artists with this background were accurate in the detail, scorning sloppy background and generalities. We can see this clearly in Concanen's cover for 'My Aesthetic Love' of 1881[27], where the designs on the plates on the itself carefully characterised dresser are detailed and not the blue blurr of a less careful artist, where the wallpaper design is systematic, and the spindly table is drawn with as much fidelity as the two people. Or in the sartorial detail of 'Dundreary's Brother Sam'[45], which contains the same information as a fashion plate of the period (1865) without the stiff formality. Again, in 'After Dark'[44], the accuracy of the railway engine would surely satisfy the most pernickety enthusiast.

It is significant that one goes to Concanen to seek out this kind of detail, and although such extras can be found in his contemporary music cover illustrators, they are not etched in with the verve that one always finds with Concanen. There is one exception—H. G. Banks[30]. Little is known of this artist except that he knew Concanen and perhaps worked with him in a group practice organised by the lithographic printers, Stannard & Dixon. In spirit he is Concanen's successor, and it is unfortunate that he was working at a time when the cover industry was in decline. He made a speciality of insets, small drawings surrounding the main subject, and worked extensively on music published by Francis, Day & Hunter (founded in 1877). Some idea of the vitality present in Banks's work can be seen from the jacket of this book.

51 (opposite)
'Come Under My Umbrella' by J. P. McArdle, a song of utter inanity, has a most curious cover by one Dodds in almost unique silhouette style. Notice the 'aesthetic' dress of the woman. The unusual typography would appear to date from the 1880s with elements from the Ringlet type (1890) and Charlemagne type (1886).

52 (overleaf)
'Prince Albert's Band March' by Stephen Glover, cover engraving by R. Branston. As 98,000 copies of this march had been published—so the legend states—there is perhaps some excuse for the apparent split in the engraving plate. Although printed in the 1850s, this cover has the naivety of an earlier age. The Glover family were inspired by the Crimean War to write a large number of pot-boiling marches, including the Sebastopol and Alma marches.

· MUSICAL ABSURDITIES ·
IN
BLACK & WHITE.

No 2.

COME UNDER MY UMBRELLA.

Written

and

Composed

By

J. F. McARDLE.

ENT. STA. HALL

LONDON.
CUNINGHAM BOOSEY & Co, 296, OXFORD STREET. W

T. PACKER IMP.

PRICE SIXPENCE

NINETY-EIGHTH THOUSAND.

PRINCE ALBERT'S BAND MARCH.

As Performed by

The Military Bands,

COMPOSED BY

STEPHEN GLOVER.

Ent. Sta. Hall.   Pr. 2s.

London :   C. Jefferys, Soho Square.   W.

PUBLISHER OF THE

QUEEN VICTORIA'S BAND MARCH........	2 0	THE PRINCE OF WALES' BAND MARCH..	2 6
PRINCE ALBERT'S BAND MARCH	2 0	HENRY THE Vth's MARCH	2 6
THE CAVALRY BAND MARCH..............	2 0	THE ROYAL SCOTCH MARCH	2 0

&c., &c., &c.

GIVE ME THY BLESSING DEAR MOTHER.

A Favorite Ballad,

Respectfully Dedicated to

ALFRED SCANLON, ESQ.RE

The Poetry & Music by

J. W. CHERRY.

By the same Author.

BEAUTIFUL IS THE SEA ...2/: | MY VILLAGE HOME........2/:
SWEET SIMPLE MELODIES...2/:

Ent: Sta. Hall.

Price 2s/:

London,

BREWER & Cº 23, BISHOPSGATE STREET WITHIN.

The most uninspired of the sheet music cover artists rarely fall below a certain level of accomplishment, as for example Dodds[51] or even the unknown Branston[52], and if one compares run of the mill covers by the minor artists with the covers of sheet music of the 1920s and 1930s it will be readily appreciated how much the art went downhill in forty years. It must be added, however, that there are sheet music covers of the 1920s and 1930s that vie with the quality productions of the Victorian period, and in fifty years' time they will be as much sought after as those of Concanen.

There is one reason for the rise of the pictorial cover that has not been discussed. This was the upsurge of interest in typography. Printers were bored with the old type faces and began experimenting with new exotics such as Tuscan Ornamented and Grotesque. Enterprising compositors realised that there was no limit to adventure in these new fields, and that they could juggle with innumerable sizes and styles to get dramatic effect [53, 54, 55, 56]. The development of display type began with the so-called 'fat faces', exaggerating the thick strokes of a letter. Although intended originally for posters, playbills and broadsides, they soon found their way into books. Hardly less influential were the Gothic types of the 1860s and 1870s, which, with innumerable variations, were used everywhere from sheet music covers to coffee-table books, and in 1880 a movement known as Artistic Printing ushered in another wide range of type.

Some of the type founts of the last half of the nineteenth century give an idea of the exuberance that permeated typography—Telegraph, Helvetian, Enchorial, Aesthetic, Japanese, Milanese, Mikado, Filigree, Corinthian, Obelisk, Sylvan, Mystic and Memorial. In the 1890s the decline of the pictorial part of the music cover went hand in hand with brash American influences on typography; a blank, it was said, was the only possible indecency in design.

The move towards a new dimension in printing was helped by the technical innovation of making type mechanically. Until 1838, type was made by hand in moulds; a skilled man could make 400 letters an hour. In that year an American invention enabled type to be made

53 (previous page)
'Give Me Thy Blessing Dear Mother' by J. W. Cherry, a very pleasantly laid-out cover in soft style.

54 (opposite)
'Wait for the Waggon' by Geo. P. Knauff. The bizarre combination of type faces, connected by delicate doodling, is a charming muddle.

WAIT FOR THE WAGGON

POPULAR SONG

COMPOSED BY

GEO. P. KNAUFF.

J. R. THOMAS'S SONGS,
in the Musical Bouquet.

Edwin P. Christy

LONDON:
MUSICAL BOUQUET OFFICE, 192, HIGH HOLBORN;
& J. ALLEN, 20, WARWICK LANE, PATERNOSTER ROW.

automatically at 100 letters a minute. The result of this is clear: the price of type fell dramatically, and printers could stock up with out of the ordinary founts that hitherto they had been unable to afford.

A refreshing wind blows through nineteenth-century typography. When ephemera such as sheet music was produced, the printers felt that they could go to town. The lettering is no longer merely informative, but becomes part of the design, as in Crowe's 'See-Saw'[57]; the text could even be incorporated into the pattern of the illustration, and type emulating branches and twigs could serve a double purpose, notifying the reader what the music was all about and serving as part of a tree to back up the art work.

There was also a great interest in three-dimensional type, and this kind of novelty infused the artists with the same sort of enthusiasm. Even when the text did not impinge on their illustrations, it was possible to counterpoint the text with their own graphic work. This led to them experimenting with lettering on their own account, as can be seen in the work of Childs.

This energy ran out towards the end of the century, coincident with the introduction of photography and new methods of colour reproduction. In the 1870s and 1880s attempts had been made to etch a photograph on metal to provide a relief surface for printing with type, but the greatest step forward was the introduction of the half-tone process. This had been projected by the photographic pioneer Fox Talbot in 1852, who suggested breaking up the tones of the photograph by means of a screen. In 1865 the idea was put forward of placing the screen in front of the sensitive plate in the camera, and from then it was only a short step to the modern half-tone process—first used by the weekly newspaper, the *Graphic*.

With imagination, photography could be the means of making music covers exciting in a new way. But instead it was used in a very dull manner; it was considered sufficient to have a photograph of the singer in a rectangle or an oval surrounded by a welter of type. The steam had gone out of sheet music cover illustration, and not until photography was disregarded did any quality return.

55 (opposite)
'Riding Thro' the Broom' by Whyte Melville and Claribel. A delightful mid-Victorian title page using a particularly appropriate form of Gothic for the song-writer's name.

RIDING THRO' THE BROOM,

SONG.

BY

Whyte Melville, Esq.re..

Set to Music

BY

CLARIBEL.

—— Price 3/- ——

London.

BOOSEY & Co 28, HOLLES STREET.

5 Collecting Sheet Music Covers

Although there are collectors of pictorial sheet music covers, they are few in number compared with, say, collectors of pot-lids or railway ephemera. This has meant that there is no generally accepted price level. About 1962 a commercial gallery put on an exhibition of Concanen covers, pricing them at from £4 to £40. This gallery, in Museum Street, Bloomsbury, has long since gone, and there is no way of finding out how many of the covers were sold. My opinion is that the covers were then overpriced. The system of pricing also seems to have been haphazard, depending not on artistry and execution but on subject-matter. In 1962 the accent was on the quaint ('Goodness, did they really have omnibuses like *that*?') and Victoriana still carried disapproving overtones.

Where is one likely to find sheet music covers? The most obvious places are music shops and second-hand bookshops, and here they are a good deal less expensive than in antique shops and shops that cater for trends, where the prices start at £5 or £6 ($12 or $14.50) for Concanen covers and go up to £40 or £50 ($96 or $120).

Those of us who have been accumulating music covers for curiosity or interest have been spoiled by the bargains we have found in the past. In 1969 I bought a bound volume of sheet music covers for £1 ($2.40); these covers included three by Concanen. This volume was discovered in a small second-hand bookshop under the railway bridge in Bexhill-on-Sea, filled with dog-eared paperbacks and odd volumes of Chambers's *Cyclopaedia*. In Eastbourne I bought for 75p ($1.80) another bound volume; there was only one Concanen, but there was also a superb Brandard and several by Maguire the younger and Hamerton.

56 (opposite)
'Who's That Tapping at the Garden Gate' by S. W. New. A neat, restrained cover using the kind of typography popular in the 1860s.

104

SUNG BY

MISS POOLE.

WHO'S THAT TAPPING

AT THE

GARDEN GATE.

SONG.

Composed by

S. W. NEW.

Ent. Sta. Hall.

PRICE 3/-

London,
HUTCHINGS & ROMER,
9, CONDUIT STREET, REGENT STREET.

"THERE'S NO ONE THERE."
Sequel to "Who's that tapping at the Garden Gate," 3/-

Most of the covers still extant are to be found in bound volumes, which were as much a part of the Victorian drawing-room scene as scrapbooks and photograph albums, and this method of keeping the covers has helped preserve them. Although the earlier covers up to about 1860 are printed on good quality paper, they are still very vulnerable when loose, and if odd pictorial covers are found in a pile of miscellaneous music, it is likely that they will be in a tatty condition.

Even when there are interesting covers in a volume of sheet music, they are sure to be outnumbered by the kind of ballads that were only sung on Sunday. These were reckoned to be serious music, and it would have been regarded as something approaching blasphemy to put a pictorial cover on them; these are not even interesting typographically, though it is curious that they are now appearing in some shops. Even at 25p (60 cents) they are outrageously expensive.

Because covers are not fine art objects, their condition is not of overwhelming importance in the present stage of music cover collecting. They are more allied to folk art and the broadsheets of half a century earlier than fine art prints. The obvious place to show wear and tear is the left-hand edge, but where the covers are intended to be framed and hung the mount will effectively hide these mishaps. It is a matter of personal taste whether a framed cover should include the printed matter, the music title, the composer's name, the singer, etc.

The first book on collecting pictorial music covers came out as long ago as 1913. This was *Illustrated Music Titles* by W. E. Imeson, a slim volume published in a limited edition at the author's expense. Imeson wrote that 'sooner or later, it will be recognized by that arbitrary mistress of arts, Dame Fashion. Then, as something to collect, it will be generally sought after.' For more than half a century Dame Fashion was very quiet about it all.

Imeson's hints on collecting were not very helpful, only serving to pad out the book. He suggested that covers could be collected according to subject—military, topical, humorous, naval, etc. With the demand for Concanen being at present so high, and therefore limiting

57 (opposite)
'See-Saw' by A. G. Crowe, with a charming anonymous cover by someone of the school of Concanen.

PERFORMED WITH THE GREATEST SUCCESS AT THE PROMENADE CONCERTS COVENT GARDEN.

SEE-SAW

STANNARD & SON.

WALTZ

COMPOSED BY

A. G. CROWE.

PIANOFORTE SOLO 2/- NET
PIANOFORTE DUET 2/6
FULL ORCHESTRA 2/-
VOCAL PART 2D.
TONIC SOL FA 2D.
MILITARY BAND & BRASS BAND ARRANGEMENTS
NOW READY

LONDON
METZLER & Co. 42, Gt MARLBOROUGH St W.

ENt STA HALL

the supply of topical covers, it would be more worth-while today to concentrate on collecting the minor artists, though there is still time to collect Brandard.

Brandard's covers for Jullien's polkas, waltzes and quadrilles have leapt in price in recent years, but he was an extraordinarily prolific artist, working in a variety of styles and media. His covers include not only humorous line engravings for the club and saloon songs, but superbly executed lithographic landscapes for drawing-room ballads and picturesque pieces. These can be purchased quite easily for as little as 25p (60 cents) each.

For covers by two artists eminently worth collecting, Maguire the younger, and Hamerton, one would not expect to pay more than £1 ($2.40) a title—and this is on the high side. It must be repeated that these are two very accomplished illustrators, and in their own way are as good as Concanen.

Although the music hall songs were directed at an urban audience, specifically a London audience, the covers are distributed all over the country and a cache of previously unissued sheet music has recently turned up in York. The provincial music hall started later than the London hall and did not really blossom until 1878 when the syndicates, formed to counter the Act which made safety curtains and a proscenium arch compulsory, began to operate, setting up chains of Hippodromes and Palaces. Therefore, covers found in the provinces are usually of a post-1878 vintage, and covers of the earlier period may well be the last relic of gay trips to sample the delights of the metropolis.

But even though there are unquestionably more music covers in the London area than in the provinces, the provinces are the places to look for bargains—and bargains there still are in this unexploited field of collect-ing. The ridiculously high prices asked by some antique dealers for sheet music covers should not put prospective collectors off, for this only proves that there is no generally accepted price level.

A very good hunting ground is the inner London suburb. The East Enders frequented the music halls but they did not buy the music; the middle-classes in the fashionable suburbs of Balham, Hornsey or Sydenham did. Their houses are being turned into flats or demolished, and such houses are repositories of history, to be cleared by the junk man or the lower echelons of the antique trade.

In London itself the antique supermarkets that have blossomed since the late 1960s are well worth a visit, especially the one behind Selfridge's in Oxford Street. Surprisingly, the antique street markets—Portobello Road on a Saturday, the Caledonian Market in Bermondsey on a Friday morning—yield little, though the Camden Passage Market in Islington is more promising. There are several shops in the Charing Cross Road area that specialise in theatrical material, and these are well worth visiting. There are two shops in Cecil Court, off Charing Cross Road, which contain a wide range of sheet music covers.

The bookshops in the Charing Cross Road are, by and large, disappointing for they have been scoured pretty well by collectors, and one must go further afield. The multitude of junk and second-hand shops in the East End are well worth investigating.

The biggest collection of music covers in Britain is that of John Hall of 17 Harrington Road, London SW7, a dealer in antiques and prints who has 50,000 covers in stock. He has been accumulating them for seventeen years. The only collection that vies with his is the theatre collection of Harvard University, USA. Also well worth a visit is Bayly's Gallery in the Princes Arcade, Piccadilly, where covers of very high quality can be found.

Covers that cost more than £8 ($19) each should be treated with suspicion, but for superb covers where the subject is interesting and specific, where the condition is fine, and which is technically unblemished, then £12–£15 ($29–36) is a reasonable price range. *Any* Concanen cover at less than £3 ($7) should be bought; Brandard covers vary widely in interest but any at less than 50p ($1.20) are worth buying; any accomplished pictorial cover at 25p (60 cents) should be purchased, even if it is unsigned (and many excellent covers are anonymous).

There are no grounds for belief that among the

anonymous covers lurk masterpieces, or that famous artists were earning pin-money through music cover illustration. Most of the anonymous illustrators were jobbing artists able to turn out capable work at short notice; it is usually found that they were employed by the lesser-known music publishers and printers, and it is likely that a good proportion of them were apprentice designers allowed a fling on a cover for a piece of sheet music that was not expected to make much money.

As for music covers in which the chief interest is typographical, then really the field is wide open. The fact that one or two antique and trendy shops are selling the most undistinguished line-engraved covers for 25p (60 cents) each is a hint of the future. It might be supposed that typographical covers have only a specialised interest, but even to those with but a perfunctory knowledge, many of these covers have an immediate aesthetic appeal. They also illuminate the times as assuredly as the best pictorial covers, from the betwigged Rustic created by Dicky Doyle in 1841 to the spiky Gothic of types of the 1870s.

There are not many fields of collecting which are virgin, and typographical sheet music covers might well capture the imagination of collectors who wish for a challenge that will not harm their pockets.

INDEX